"*Custom Scars* is a powerful story that many in
will relate to. Steve's trials are significant, but
Ultimately, we can't control our bodies but we c
break us or build us. Whether your scars are on the outside from surgeries, or on the inside from
depression, anxiety, or stress, you'll be able to relate to what Steve has been through."

> — Maya Brown-Zimmerman
> Blogger at *Musings of a Marfan Mom*
> Administrator of Marfan Syndrome Facebook Page

"Steve Henry is among the toughest individuals I know. *Custom Scars* is his story. He is
acquainted with scars - visible and invisible; physical and emotional.

But, as tough as Steve is, he is a pastor with a tender heart. "Pastor Steve" loves Jesus with all his
heart, soul, mind and strength. He is called to serve others and does so by pointing folks in pain
to Christ - who Himself is acquainted with sorrow, grief, and pain (Isaiah 53).

He will encourage you with his authenticity, wit, and winsomeness. If you've ever wondered if
there is hope for healing, encouragement for enduring, or empowerment for overcoming, then
tune your ears to Steve as he tells you his story...and then, turn your eyes upon Jesus."

> — Todd H. Fetters
> Bishop, Church of the United Brethren in Christ

"*Custom Scars* is a captivating memoir of Steve Henry, a pastor with Marfan syndrome, first
diagnosed at a tender age of twelve years. The author has depicted how he continues to battle to
overcome both the external scars of multiple lifesaving surgeries and also a myriad of emotional
scars that he has sustained since his early childhood. His account of his medical and personal
ordeals is uncannily intimate and will connect with any reader, for it describes so poignantly the
concerns anyone may have when encountering a lifelong medical diagnosis. His title is apt as this
metaphor pervades his journey but leaves an ultimately positive, inspiring, and uplifting message
of how his faith allowed him to mold his scars into immeasurable strengths. Mr. Henry's journey
through his medical hurdles, elegantly depicted in his account, continues to inspire me
professionally and personally."

> — Dr. Suneeta Madan-Khetarpal
> Medical Genetics – Children's Hospital of Pittsburgh

"I first met Steve when he showed up at Bible College as a eighteen-year-old freshman. Steve
had just been discharged from the hospital where he had open-heart surgery on his teenage body.

I watched Steve grow into a Godly man and leader of men during his college years and
beyond. His warmth, extroversion, and quick sense of humor endear this gentle giant to everyone
he meets.

I know Steve. I love him. I know the truth of his incredible journey. Enjoy the humor, passion
and enthusiasm Steve has for life as he tells his story and let it be an agent of God's grace to
further His transformation in you!"

> — Dr. John Neihof
> President of Wesley Biblical Seminary

Custom Scars

WHERE HOPE CAN BE FOUND IN THE MIDST OF PAIN

Steve Henry

Custom Scars is dedicated to my children:
Michaela, Corban, Dylan, Andrew, & Jana.

May you never walk away from the hope that is
found through Jesus Christ.

CONTENTS

I have worked much harder, been in prison more frequently, been flogged more severely, and been exposed to death again and again. Five times I received from the Jews the forty lashes minus one. Three times I was beaten with rods, once I was stoned, three times I was shipwrecked, I spent a night and a day in the open sea, I have been constantly on the move. I have been in danger from rivers, in danger from bandits, in danger from my own countrymen, in danger from Gentiles; in danger in the city, in danger in the country, in danger at sea; and in danger from false brothers. I have labored and toiled and have often gone without sleep; I have known hunger and thirst and have often gone without food; I have been cold and naked. Besides everything else, I face daily the pressure of my concern for all the churches. Who is weak, and I do not feel weak? Who is led into sin, and I do not inwardly burn?

Apostle Paul
2 Corinthians 11:23-29

FOREWORD

On March 21, 2014, at just thirty-three years old, I was diagnosed with stage-three breast cancer that had spread to my lymph nodes. This event completely caught me off guard. I have no family history of cancer and consider myself a very active and healthy person. That was the beginning of a whirlwind of events that lasted over two years. At first, my husband and I drove back and forth to Fox Chase Cancer Center in Philadelphia, three-and-a-half hours from our home in Central Pennsylvania, seven times for appointments. Exactly one month after being diagnosed, on Good Friday, I had a double mastectomy and began reconstruction surgery. After another month of recovery, I began a rigorous regimen of eight chemotherapy treatments, which required more long road trips, one every other week, that lasted through the summer.

After letting my body recover from those treatments, I had a final surgery to complete my reconstruction. I then began radiation treatments in order to lessen my risk for reoccurrence. Since I tested positive for the BRCA-2 gene mutation, I had a full hysterectomy, which also lessened my chance of reoccurrence or of getting other cancers.

Having two young boys who were seven and two at the time of my diagnosis, I knew I needed to fight for my life. They were much too young to truly understand the severity of cancer, and my motherly instinct wanted to protect them from needing to worry about me. This task proved to be especially difficult, however, on those days I felt like I was physically and emotionally falling apart, like when my two-year-old got a surprise ear infection or had a total breakdown because he couldn't get his glove on his hand, or when my seven-year-old, who is never sick, vomited on my bedroom carpet the day before I was scheduled to have major surgery. Sometimes during this journey, I found myself telling God that I cannot fight cancer and take care of my family at the same time. By His grace, however, I made it through. I am also thankful that many of these moments are now beginning to feel like distant memories.

The scars I have are real. They hurt. They make me sad. They make me cry. They make me angry. Some days they honestly make me a little depressed. But while my scars from surgery stripped me of some of my womanly image, and the chemo temporarily took away my eyebrows, eyelashes, and long blonde hair, they have also opened doors for me and changed my life. These scars have reminded me that true beauty is found deeper than our human shell. They have made me more sensitive to the people suffering around me and made me closer to my Savior and the Creator of the universe who loves me. My scars have made me bold and more excited to share my faith. Even though I have scars from this earth, I serve a God who has overcome my scars and has given me grace and the gift of eternal life through the scars on His son's hands.

Sometimes I wish we didn't need to have the scars of this earth. Sometimes the pain seems bigger than I am and I feel completely overcome. I truly believe, however, the pain and struggles we face here can direct us to the One who is bigger than ourselves. I have found that, during some of my weakest moments, I have become closer to my Savior. If it weren't for those moments of helplessness, I truly believe my sinful human nature would lead me to believe I could make it through life on my own. Through this process, God has reminded me I was created by and for Him. Even though I love my family to the point I would give my own life for them, I still was not created for them.

I have known Steve Henry all my life. He's my older cousin and the houses we grew up in were only a few miles apart. I have always known about his health difficulties and his countless surgeries. Until reading this book, however, I had never heard him talk so deeply about his life story. He has made himself so vulnerable to others by showing how his *Custom Scars* have shaped him into the man he is today.

This book is about Steve's scars, but the truth of the matter is we all have some type of scar. Some, like Steve, have many scars and others may not have that many yet. The question I'd like to ask is do we let our scars define us, or do we persevere through our scars and allow them to shape us and make us into stronger people? Do we find a way to turn bad scars around for the good of our families and our stories?

I recommend this book to anyone who has scars, whether you have overcome your scars, whether you let your scars define you, or whether your scars are still healing. Steve's story tells of a physically and spiritually strong man who decided not to let any of his physical struggles get in the way of leading a life that seeks to be used in big ways. I urge you to dive into this book and allow Steve's journey to be an encouragement to you. Please do not let yourselves be overcome by your struggles, because there is hope amidst our scars and there is One who has Scars that Save.

- April Lee Williams

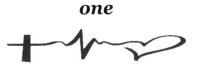

one

HOPE IN THE MIDST OF SCARS

"You still have to shower!" my wife, Amanda, told me as I casually ate my supper on May 27, 2016. I had completely forgotten to shower that day and we had less than an hour to be ready for our kids' end-of-the-school-year program. Frantically I rushed my empty dinner plate into the kitchen, grabbed some clean clothes from the bedroom, and jumped under the streaming water of the shower.

After washing as quickly as possible, I started to rinse the soap off, but as I raised my right arm, extreme pain shot through my upper back. Excruciating pain that I had never felt before — but I knew without a doubt what had happened. *I just had a dissection, my aorta just tore! This isn't good. Every heartbeat is pumping blood into my chest cavity. I'm bleeding out inside.*

Anticipating a hospital trip, I struggled to wash my hair and then called for Amanda. Breathing was hard, the pain was intense, and I could hardly stand. I assumed that in a matter of minutes I would be dead from internal blood loss. Hoping for the best but preparing for the worst, I still needed to get to the hospital five miles away. Staggering in pain, I could only muster enough strength to put on a pair of shorts and then Amanda, with all five kids, somehow managed to load me into the van and off to the hospital we sped.

Once we arrived at the emergency room, I turned around and looked at my beautiful children with tears starting to fill my eyes. I

1

knew this was going to be the last time they would see me alive. Gazing into each of their eyes, I told them all "I love you" with tears now flowing from mine.

Amanda came around the van to open my door. I glanced back one last time at the kids before entering the ER. My heart told me that was my final goodbye; my wife was becoming a widow and my five children becoming fatherless at the ages of fourteen, eleven, ten, seven, and five. I knew that a majority of people never survive an aortic dissection, and I started to internally and emotionally prepare for death and heaven.

At the registration counter I told the receptionist that I had Marfan syndrome and had just had an aortic dissection. As plain as I could, I stressed that promptness of treatment was imperative for my survival. After struggling to give her my information, someone sitting in the ER waiting room actually helped me to a wheelchair in the hallway. The receptionist then told someone (maybe the nurse?), "This young man is complaining of back pain, it might just be kidney stones." I was irate. I was only in the ER a couple of minutes alone before Amanda was by my side. I was still sitting in the wheelchair in the hallway with minimal urgency for care. I told Amanda what had been said about the kidney stones and told her that if I died in that chair that she was to sue them for as much as she could get. (I'm not the suing type, but if they leave me sitting here to die in a wheelchair, at least my family will have some financial help.)

Thankfully a cardiologist from a larger hospital was in the ER that day and heard the words "Marfan," "previous surgeries," and "dissection" and got me back stat. Hence a miraculous but painful journey for our family was about to begin.

That was day one of my sixty-nine-day hospital and rehabilitation journey. That was day one of me not preaching for over 130 days. That day one changed the course of our lives forever.

~ᴧ~ᴧ~ᴧ~

Romans 15:13 says, "May the God of hope fill you with all joy and peace as you trust in him, so that you may overflow with hope by the power of the Holy Spirit." It's hard to find hope when your life crashes to pieces. Life is composed of emotional and physical scars that often make us feel hopeless. None of us should give up, but that is definitely easier said than done.

I've wanted to give up on countless occasions because my scars cut too deep. One of my Marfan-related procedures produced an incision which stretched from below my belly button on my left side all the way up around to my left shoulder blade. The pain from that procedure alone was enough for me to want to throw my hands in the air and just give up. I told my wife, "I just want to die so you and Michaela (she was our only child then) can find another husband/father who is healthy." Amanda reassured me with all her heart that they both needed me alive. Through her love and words of the great hymn "It Is Well," my hope started to restore. I've been there, lying facedown in the valley, not able to get any lower.

~ᴧ~ᴧ~ᴧ~

Two words used frequently throughout these pages will be *scars* and *hope*. Everyone has scars. They could be physical, emotional, or even spiritual scars. In the midst of these scars I believe that we also need hope. Hope that we are created for a purpose. Hope that we can be accepted by others and by God regardless of our scars. The

3

scars that we all have are unique, so they are our *Custom Scars* . . . hence the title.

The scars that have accumulated in my life are mostly due to being diagnosed with a genetic condition called Marfan syndrome. Being diagnosed with this when I was twelve has given me an invaluable perspective on how to have hope when life seems so dark and unfair. My scars,

> **My scars will not control me because I have allowed Christ to be the one in control.**

physical and emotional, have never been enjoyable to face, but over the last forty years they have been instrumental in molding me into the son, husband, father, and pastor that I am today. Philippians 4:13 states, "I can do everything through him who gives me strength." My scars will not control me because I have allowed Christ to be the one in control.

The deep scars of being bullied, losing a parent to death as a teenager, having significant physical restrictions, wondering if someone would love me, and also having two of our five children inherit my genetic condition have been a part of my life. Although those scars will always be with me, they won't control me.

My prayer is that after reading my story, you will use your *Custom Scars* to help others in need of hope. You are alive for a reason. God has a perfect purpose for your life. Regardless of your scars, you are a special person and have been uniquely and wonderfully made by God. (Jeremiah 29:11)

I wonder why we so often allow our scars to get in the way of accomplishing great things. Are we afraid we won't be strong enough to see greatness in ourselves or to see a task through to its

4

completion? Have we allowed society to label us as inferior or weak because of our scars? Why do we so often allow our scars to dictate our lives? Those are real questions that everyone who is reading this has asked themselves.

Trust me, you weren't born a mistake. It doesn't matter how many scars you have, you are made perfect through God. God knew you before you were born! In Jeremiah 1:5 the prophet Jeremiah wrote about the Lord knowing him before he was formed in his mother's womb. Your life is valuable because you are created in the image of God. No matter what circumstances have occurred in your life to produce your *Custom Scars*, God can use them for good. He made you exactly the way He wanted you to be, and He has an incredible plan for your life just waiting for you. All you have to do is ask. My heart's deepest desire is that you will experience hope for yourself and also use your story to offer hope to others.

two

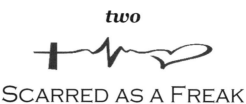

SCARRED AS A FREAK

Life for me outside of the womb started on Valentine's Day, 1978 in rural northwestern Pennsylvania. (I share the date of my birth with my maternal and paternal grandfathers, as well as my great-great-grandfather. Albeit none of them are still living, I always enjoy sharing that factoid since other family members "share" birthdays. This is important to know later in the story.)

Before my first birthday, my parents noticed that my feet weren't developing correctly. After they consulted the family doctor, he informed them that my feet were angling inward and needed to be corrected for my legs and feet to develop properly. Learning to crawl wasn't easy as I had to learn with both of my feet in heavy casts. My father remembers how pitiful I looked while dragging my casts behind me. Apparently, I was starting off on the wrong foot from the earliest of ages.

The casts were removed after a few months and I was up and running. Each year Mom took me to the shoe store to buy a high-quality, supportive pair of church/school shoes to ensure proper foot support and growth. I imagine it was hard for my parents to see their son dragging his legs behind him, so the investment in proper footwear was an easy decision.

My mother stayed home and took care of me and my older sister, Becky, trying her best to keep us in line. Mom was always there for us. She took her parenting responsibilities seriously and desired her children to make the right decisions in life. My mother grew up with dysfunctional parents, so bringing children into the world was quite scary for her. My mother had a lot of hopelessness in her childhood and she didn't want that for her kids. She wanted to give Becky and me the parental love and care that was void in her upbringing. She was a staunch disciplinarian and I am very thankful for that as an adult.

My mother carried the scars of self-doubt. Her older sister was the main parent figure in her life and their bond was very strong. They relied on each other and their loving relationship helped keep my mom sane!

Homelife was okay other than the fact that my mom and dad didn't really get along. The arguments my parents had with each other were never pleasant to watch or hear. Both of them had anger and bitterness issues they needed to address. Sadly that didn't happen until the final days of my mom's life. I knew both my parents loved me and would do anything for me, but I didn't grow up in a household where a good marriage was exemplified. I, like many children, did not see my parents showing affection to each other. I saw two people who were together for reasons that weren't very clear to me. Was this what marriage was supposed to be?

By the time I was five, I knew I wasn't like other kids. My body was shaped differently; I was incredibly thin and significantly taller than everyone in my class. My chest didn't look like theirs either. Mine was concave, and my mother always encouraged me to keep my shirt on so kids wouldn't tease me about its shape.

On top of that, I was a sensitive kid. I had a hard time emotionally when kids teased me, which was practically every day.

Day after day, week after week, I came home from school crying because of the verbal torments of the kids. My elementary years were filled with being teased and bullied for looking different (and being REALLY sensitive). My mother was my rock and support when the waves of pain rolled into my life. We all need someone as an anchor.

The crazy thing is that I went to a very small Christian school and I was still picked on mercilessly. Actually, the worst bullying that ever happened to me was at church. One Wednesday evening when I was eight years old, a twelve-year-old boy was chasing me. I ran into a Sunday school classroom and cowered to the floor between a big curtain and a file cabinet. The bully found me hiding and started throwing markers and crayons down on my head. All I could do was curl up in a ball and cry.

I think back on that experience and my heart goes out to kids who are dealing with being bullied for just being themselves. Could I help that I was skinny? Could I help that I was sensitive? I have to admit I could be a little annoying, but I was just a boy trying to figure out how to live life. It always seems like a bully is lurking around every corner.

(Ironically, that bully grew up to be a pastor. Eight years ago, he and his family actually stayed in our home and took care of it for a couple of days during Thanksgiving break while we were out of town. It is wonderful how God can change people's hearts and lives.)

Crayons and markers are one thing, but pants are a whole different arena. One day during elementary recess a group of guys chased me down in the middle of the baseball field. Once I was caught, they proceeded to remove my pants and then ran away with them! Honestly, I can't remember how that one got resolved, but I'm sure I got my pants back by the end of the day. Experiences like those create scars in our lives, memories we wish we could erase from our minds but, sadly, they are etched into the fabric of our being.

Maybe you were bullied when you were younger and can understand these feelings and scars. As a father, I do everything I can to shield my kids from these types of assaults, but they are everywhere. I know my children have already experienced ridicule and teasing, and when this happens, we not only support our children, but we also direct them to God's promises. Psalm 10:17-18a says, "You hear, O LORD, the desire of the afflicted; you encourage them, and you listen to their cry, defending the fatherless and the oppressed." I regret not looking to God as a child; instead, I looked to my mother for all my strength. Regardless of your age, looking to God for strength and hope is always best.

Regardless of your age, looking to God for strength and hope is always best.

I was different. My parents, especially my mom, did everything in her power to reassure me that I was loved. My mother was my greatest support; she was the one who was always there for me. If the weather outside was nice, my dad worked sunup to sundown and wasn't home much, so I gravitated more toward my mom during those pivotal early elementary years when I really needed to be more connected with my father.

My parents always knew I was physically different from other boys. Although my family knew my bone structure was a little different than everyone else's, it wasn't until a family reunion when I was twelve that a relative spoke to my father about someone she knew who had a child with many of the same physical features as I. She cautiously informed him the child had a heart condition. She recommended I be evaluated by specialists. The relative told my father that if I had something called Marfan syndrome, our family must take it seriously.

I can't even imagine what my parents were thinking or feeling when that family member mentioned I might have a serious health condition. I just thought a doctor would perform some tests, everything would come back clear, and I would go on with my life as normal. Besides, the teasing had substantially decreased by this point in my life because I was close to being six feet tall and fairly good at sports.

Nonetheless, my parents made an appointment at Children's Hospital in Pittsburgh and we headed two hours south for testing and genetic counseling. This was the first time I had ever been in a really large hospital. My life revolved around small-town living and going to the doctor was almost like going to a relative's house. Our family doctor and his staff knew the folks in our rural community by name, so going to Pittsburgh for a hospital trip was definitely eye-opening. Little did I know this would be the first of many trips to the hospitals in the 'Burgh.

The specialists ran some tests and I met with a very kind geneticist. After the doctor had a long dialogue with my parents about our family history, and after I spent a bit of time standing stark naked in front of this guy (maybe having my pants taken off in a baseball field prepared me for this?) the doctor told my parents. . .

YOUR SON IS A FREAK MUTATION!

Honestly, that wasn't all he said, but as a twelve-year-old boy, that was all I heard. The doctor concluded I indeed had a condition called Marfan syndrome. He termed it a freak mutation because he could not find any evidence I had inherited it from my parents. Instead, the mutation of a protein called fibrillin-1 that causes Marfan syndrome happened to me because of a freak mutation, not because of something I inherited. (It is referred to more commonly now as a spontaneous mutation.) Even though "freak mutation" wasn't the most encouraging words the geneticist could have used, they were the best description of how I ended up with this condition. All I knew was my life would never be the same.

My parents asked the doctor what my life expectancy was and whether my condition would affect my daily activities. While he explained that I would never be able to play contact sports or do many other physically strenuous activities, he assured them that as long as they kept my regular doctor appointments, my life expectancy should be the same as those without Marfan syndrome. A cardiologist would also need to monitor the condition of my aorta yearly. Marfan syndrome often causes the aorta, the main artery supplying oxygenated blood to the circulatory system, to enlarge and tear. At this point my aorta was normal size and no significant alarms arose during that first doctor's appointment. I began taking a

11

beta-blocker to help keep my heart from overexerting as a precaution. I didn't realize the full impact of that day's diagnosis until the summer after I graduated high school.

Marfan syndrome is a connective tissue disorder that affects roughly 1 in 5,000 people. (www.marfan.org/about/marfan) Since connective tissue joins nearly everything in our bodies, the doctor examined my skeletal structure, joints, flexibility, spine, eyes, and aorta. Of everything in my body, my aorta has been affected the most. When I was first diagnosed, the goal was to prevent wear on my aorta for as long as possible with the hope of prolonging its lifespan. Oftentimes when someone is diagnosed with Marfan syndrome, his or her aorta can become thin, stretched, and tear with exertion. The walls of the aorta can thin out, increasing the risk of an aneurysm. The aortic valve can also become enlarged and in need of replacement.

So as a preteen, I had an aorta that could burst at any time (at least those were my thoughts) and, of course, I was a "freak mutation." What a day at the doctor's office! I wonder what my parents were thinking when we drove home from the hospital that day?

⎯⎯ᴧ⎯ᴧ⎯ᴧ⎯

So now what? You may have asked that same question when you received news like this about a health condition or when a close friend or loved one received similar news. It boils down to how this condition actually affects my day-to-day living. Maybe you were diagnosed with multiple sclerosis, cancer, diabetes, or any number of physical conditions or diseases. You've had to ask the tough questions, and oftentimes the answers aren't what you want to hear. When people say, "Everything's going to be all right" it doesn't help because they've not walked in your shoes.

Amidst the pain of our scars, the promises of God still hold true whether we accept them or not. Psalm 33:22 says, "May your unfailing love rest upon us, O LORD, even as we put our hope in you." God's love is so vast that regardless of the physical *Custom Scars* in our lives, we can place our hope in Him. Even with that hope, we still have to face each day with our scars that typically change everything in our life.

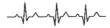

This diagnosis changed the dynamics with my father since he operated heavy equipment. I was around heavy objects and performed manual work as a child for his business. But could I still do this now? Should I do this now? This was all new for me and especially for my parents. My dad had always worked hard to provide for the family, but that line of work wasn't healthy for my body. Dad was probably at a loss sometimes, wondering if I should or shouldn't do something.

One thing I know is that my parents loved me just as much as they did before I was diagnosed. Most parents want a perfectly healthy baby. For many, if there is even a chance their unborn child has a genetic condition, such as Down's syndrome, they elect to abort the unborn baby. This breaks my heart because all life is meaningful and deserves to be loved. In Psalm 139:14 God says that while we were still inside our mother's womb, He knew us and we are fearfully and wonderfully made. God doesn't make mistakes.

My parents loved me for who I was regardless of my limitations. I believe beyond a shadow of doubt that if they had known I would be born with a genetic condition, they still would have chosen life. All life is special and God has a purpose for us all, regardless of any "freak mutations." Never devalue someone who isn't "normal" in your eyes. That person is just as special and valued by God as you are and deserves life.

By the time I was old enough to begin my freshman year in high school, the small Christian school I attended closed, so I started attending a larger Christian school in a nearby town. By this time I was six feet three, athletic, and the teasing had stopped. I had developed a little tougher skin and became the class clown of sorts.

So as a fourteen-year old I entered a larger school where they had a sports program. Being tall, I really enjoyed basketball! I joke around now that I love the sport because the basketball rim is so low it's easy to put a little ball through it. But even though I can have fun with this now, during that first year in high school, my heart longed to be on the basketball court.

I remember sitting on the top bleacher during the basketball games, cheering, clapping, and crying. I cheered and clapped when our team was winning or made a great play. I cried when our team was losing and all I wanted to do was suit up and help them win. I knew I could help! I knew I was better than the other team's big man underneath the hoop. I knew I could block most of his shots, but here I was sitting, longing, heartbroken, and crying.

I sat on those top bleachers for many games, struggling with the emotions and pain of being a "freak mutation." One girl, Amy, whom I had known from church for years, routinely sat beside me, put her arm around me, and encouraged me. She was a friend when I really needed one. Just her presence beside me, letting me know that I was still important even though I couldn't be on the court, helped me through those tough times that year. I don't know if she remembers, but just as you remember the scars when you were cornered in a church between a file cabinet and a curtain, when others have taken your pants, or when someone calls you a "freak mutation," you remember the care and concern that someone freely offers you. You remember when someone offers you a word of hope.

You remember when someone offers you a word of hope.

Scars accumulate over time. My pain was accumulating because of the scars in my life, and the pain of sitting on the bleachers was adding even more scars. This first year of high school was the hardest year for me emotionally, but I am thankful for friends like Amy who helped me carry my burden. After that first year of watching from the bleachers, I was given the opportunity for the rest of my high school years to be the water boy (tallest one in the league) and to even help coach the junior varsity basketball team my senior year. That inclusion made me feel part of the team even though I never put on a jersey.

I wonder how often we love folks unconditionally regardless of their scars? When have we reached out and put our arms around a hurting person like Amy did for me?

You may have been bullied when you were a child for not being "normal." Maybe you have substantially large ears, a differently formed chest, oddly long fingers, really crooked teeth, nearsightedness, or hips that make it hard for pants to stay up! (All those things describe me.) If you can relate to any or all of my differences, or if you have other differences in your outward appearance, let me encourage you again: God loves you and you are not a mistake.

It was hard to be different from the other kids, but I wouldn't change my differences for anything. I wouldn't change any of my physical and emotional pain for one day of being "normal." How God made me is my normal and He made me exactly the way I am supposed to be. I thank Him for my uniqueness. You need to thank Him for your uniqueness, too.

Life as a child and young teenager wasn't easy, but I've been able to use those scars to help others who may have similar experiences to mine. I know what it is like to be a child who doesn't fit in, and I know what it is like to have children who have the same genetic condition as their father. I know it's not going to be easy for my children, but I will be right beside them each step of the way.

Until the summer of 1993, my life wasn't the easiest, but through the love of my parents, my family, and my church family, I survived. Little did I know that life doesn't typically get easier and the most difficult trial would happen when I was just fifteen years old.

CUSTOM SCARS & CUSTOM CARS

Throughout my childhood my father was always working on one or two classic or custom car projects. The first car I remember him

16

buying was a 1957 Chevy Nomad when I was in early elementary school. I had never been in a car that was as long as that Nomad. It was painted metallic gold with some very inappropriate graphics painted on the hood and back hatch.

It took dad a few years to restore that Nomad and then, ten years later, he sold it to a gentleman in California.

During my teen years, Dad built a 1955 Chevy step-side pickup, and I remember bolting the wooden bed of that truck onto the frame. But at the end of most chapters in *Custom Scars* I'm going to be focusing on my dad's pride and joy car: his 1948 Ford Sedan that he still has today.

My father restored the Nomad and the pickup to similar conditions as they would have looked originally. This Ford Sedan (pictured on the cover) was going to be different.

Dad wasn't going to strip it all down to its nuts and bolts and then rebuild it to look like the original. No, my dad was going to make this his *Custom Car*. Nothing was going to be "normal" about it. He wanted a different engine, interior, exterior, suspension, roof, and many other customizations. It was going to be the way my father wanted it to be.

I trust you understand where I'm going with this comparison. I may not be "normal" because of my *Custom Scars*, but who I am is exactly how my heavenly "Father" wants me to be. This is how the Master Designer created me.

These customizations don't make me unloving or ugly. Just as my dad was going to build this *Custom Car* from the bottom up with all its uniqueness and customizations, God has a perfect plan for all of us and will put our life pieces together if we will allow Him. He will use our *Custom Scars* to build us exactly how He wants us to be.

three

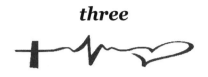

THE SCARS OF DEATH

As you know, my mother grew up in a home that wasn't the most supportive, and she was basically raised by her sister, Nancy, my aunt. The two of them were best friends and talked on the phone frequently. Each summer our vacation found us at Aunt Nancy and Uncle Don's house in Erie, Pennsylvania. My dad stayed home to work, so it was always Mom, Becky, and me who vacationed for a week. We typically found ourselves in three "staple" places each year. The first was Lake Erie, where I was positive a shark was going to jump out and eat me while I was on a boat ride. Next was Waldameer Amusement Park, where the haunted house scared me so badly one summer that I jumped on my aunt's back and she carried me the rest of the way through it. (I never went into that place again!) Finally, we always went to the zoo. Each year I measured myself to see if I was as tall as the giraffes.

My mom and Aunt Nancy shared a genuine sisterly love. Mom drew great strength from that love. Aunt Nancy was a vital part of our family's life even though she lived a couple of hours away. She was my mom's best friend, and they laughed and loved to share life together as much as they could.

During my freshman year of high school, and my sister's senior year, my mother was diagnosed with Hodgkin's disease . . . cancer. She had cancer many years before this, but during my freshman year she started chemo and radiation treatments for this second

19

round. Being so young, fifteen, I didn't know the full ramifications of cancer and just assumed that Mom would be fine after a few months of treatments.

I still lived like I typically did, and to me, Mom's treatments appeared to be working. Becky frequently took Mom to her treatments, but I now know that they kept the seriousness of her cancer from me. My sister was so strong during this time and cared for many of Mom's needs. Because both my mom and sister looked to the Lord to renew their strength, they were able to run and not grow weary, and walk and not be faint, as Isaiah 40:31 says. That kind of strength only comes from the Lord.

During the second half of my freshman year, Mom was frequently in and out of the hospital. I still assumed she would make it back home and life would be normal again. (I learned through this experience the importance of being honest with my own children about my health condition and the health of those we love. It is part of preparing them for the realities they will experience throughout life. Our family discusses what happens when someone dies, because a person's eternal destiny is important to our family, and our Christian faith speaks in great depths about where a soul goes after an earthly body dies.)

One day, during the spring of 1993, my mother and I were alone in the house. Mom was upstairs and I was playing video games in the basement. I had one of the original Nintendo's and was busy playing a ninja game. For those of you who remember, many of these older gaming systems didn't save a game at different checkpoints. So beating the game required playing the entire game in one sitting. So I was playing this game in the basement for hours when I heard something from upstairs that didn't sound normal.

Turning the volume down, perturbed, I listened to hear what might have been the problem. It was my mother yelling for me to get upstairs. Pressing pause (at least I could do that), I ran upstairs. But where was Mom? I couldn't find her! I yelled, "Where are you?"

I heard a reply, "I'm in here!"

As I ran through the house, trying to find my mother, I located her in the bathroom that was connected to my parents' bedroom. She was lying on the floor in severe pain, unable to pull her pants back up after using the toilet. Her body was in such pain due to the cancer that she had to lie on the floor and call for help. She told me to get a bath towel and cover her up, which I did.

Still unable to move because of the pain, she thanked me, while still trying to protect me, and told me she would be fine and that I could go back downstairs to my game. At that moment, I knew I wasn't ready for the direction my life was taking. So I just "tuned out reality" and went back to my game.

There was so much that could have been done differently to prepare me for what was going to happen. I was often told that things were going to be fine under the guise of protecting me. I needed someone to share with me reality and not the false hope that was so often spoken. Life was shattering into pieces and I felt very alone. I needed someone to come alongside of me to walk with me through this pain. Lamentations 3:21 and 24 speak of God being all we need and that we can be hopeful in Him. My scars from watching my mother battle cancer could have healed differently if my relationship with God would have been encouraged and developed

21

with total hope through Him. I was just a fifteen-year-old kid with Marfan syndrome who couldn't do what many of my friends could. But now what was really happening to the person I loved the most?

As has been stated, my parents didn't have the greatest relationship. They were both Christians but had many skeletons in their closets they had never dealt with. Trust, communication, intimacy, and a host of other things were void in their marriage. The bitterness they had toward one another festered year after year. My mother even made her own bedroom in the basement, where she slept so she could still be in the same house without being in the same bedroom as my father. Truth be known, my parents stayed together primarily for the sake of my sister and me.

Many evenings while Mom was watching television, I laid my head on her lap while she rubbed my back, telling me how much she loved me and encouraged me to be strong. I vividly remember her touch, a touch that has been void in my life for over twenty-five years. I miss it so much. I not only heard love coming from Mom's lips, but I felt the love from the touch of her hands.

My mom always told me, "Stephen, don't grow up to be like your father." I can't imagine how my dad would have felt if, at that time, he knew she was telling me that. Honestly, my dad worked to escape from the heavy burdens of homelife, so I could understand why Mom would feel that way. Is change even possible when years of hurt have layered one scar on top of another? I didn't have much hope that anything would ever change.

Becky graduated from high school in June 1993, but Mom wasn't able to attend her graduation because she was in the hospital. I honestly don't know how my sister managed to make it through that day. I can't imagine attending my high school graduation knowing my mom couldn't attend because she was in the hospital less than ten miles away. Mom was just too sick.

As June passed and July came, Mom was in the hospital more than she was at home. We visited her at the cancer center regularly, though I had a hard time visiting with her. I wanted to see her, but I still believed the treatments were going to work and she would be able to come home. That false hope was still holding strong. I couldn't understand why we were making so many trips if she was going to be coming home.

Aunt Nancy was with Mom in the hospital more than I was. She was with us kids just about every day, too. Aunt Nancy loved my sister and me as if we were her own children! I know her heart was breaking, knowing we were going to have to say goodbye to our mother and that she was going to lose her best friend.

During the first days of July, my mother asked God what He wanted her to do about the strained relationship between her and my dad. God revealed to her that she had to let go of the bitterness toward my father. Miraculously she did. She told my father that she no longer had the memories of all the hurt and bitterness and that she only remembered the good times they had together. Then she told him she was praying for that same experience in his life.

After that conversation, my mom was in a fairly regular comatose state. Every time we went to see her from that point forward, she wasn't responsive. Meanwhile, I was trying to prepare for what I wasn't prepared for, and my dad didn't have any idea how to raise a fifteen-year-old son and a seventeen-year-old daughter by himself.

Miraculously on July 15 my mother was wide awake, fairly pain-free, and had a clear mind! I remember talking to her that day and believing once again that everything was going to be fine. I was positive God had healed her and we would be home again as a family! But as we all know, death is inevitable, and my mother would soon meet her Savior.

During that day when Mom was alert, unbeknownst to me, Mom and Dad both let the bitterness go and forgave each other of all the mistakes, attitudes, and venom they had thrust upon one another for so many years. That was the day they forgave twenty-four years of bitterness and anger-filled marriage and desired a new start.

Psalm 130:7 says, "O Israel, put your hope in the LORD, for with the LORD is unfailing love and with him is full redemption." My parents both sought the hope and love of God and experienced full redemption in their marriage. Even during the eleventh hour, our scars can at least begin healing due to the mighty power of God.

Mom told Dad, "Lester, if God chooses to heal me, we will start over and make sure this marriage is done right, but if God doesn't choose to heal me, then go out and find another wife and treat her how she should be treated. Don't make the same mistakes twice." Some of her final words were words of forgiveness and I am sure they concluded their conversation that day with "I love you."

She also stressed for Dad to take care of me because of my health concerns. She fought so hard to live for her kids, but by this time, she knew it was going to be up to Dad and God to see us through this next step in our lives. As 1 John 4:4 states that greater is He [Jesus] that is in me, than he [Satan] that is in the world.

By the conclusion of that day, each person in our family had spent quality time with Mom and the scars of a bad marriage had been miraculously forgiven.

The following morning, July 16, 1993, we visited Mom and she was back in a comatose state. The day that I believed was the "miracle day," when I thought Mom was getting better and going to come home, didn't happen as I was hoping it would. Looking back, though, it was a miracle day because forgiveness happened and my mother and father were able to have the peace that surpasses all understanding, as well as closure for what was about to come.

We knew it was a matter of days or even hours until she would be gone. Aunt Nancy was at the hospital with us as she normally was. At lunchtime Dad took us kids out for something to eat. We were only gone for forty-five minutes, but when we got back to the cancer center, I remember a feeling of hush and sadness throughout the building when we walked through the doors. Sorrow was evident on the faces of the nurses as we started walking towards Mom's room. After making a right turn down the hallway to where Mom's room was, Aunt Nancy came out to meet us.

"Your mom's gone," she said with tears in her eyes. I glanced into the room and only saw my mother's legs and feet under her sheets. I wish now that I had gone into her room to see her just one last time, but I stood in the hall, not knowing what to do. The person in my life who loved me so unconditionally, who protected me when I was being bullied, who gave me hope when I didn't see any hope, was gone . . . forever.

I didn't know how I was supposed to act. How was I supposed to feel? What in the world was going to happen in my life? Was I supposed to cry? Yell? Was I supposed to sit? Stand? What was I supposed to do?

I walked into the waiting room/lounge area and sat down. One of the nurses came over and put her arm around me. I can't remember if she said anything, but I know she was there for me to cry on. I don't know how Becky, my dad, or Aunt Nancy processed this or reacted to the loss of Mom. I am sure they were as lost as I was. At the age of forty-seven, Beverly Lynne Henry, my mother, was gone, taken by cancer.

It wasn't long until we left that building, never to see Mom again on this earth. The emptiness and absolute void in my heart is indescribable to this day. Only those who've suffered a similar trauma can understand the emptiness of losing a parent as a teen.

My mother was cremated and the funeral service was incredible, not that I really remember what was said, but so many people came out to support our family. The funeral home so was packed with people that many of our family and friends had to stand or sit in other rooms, not even able to see what was going on. A majority of my classmates and their families attended the service as well. That kind of support was vital during this time.

So how was I supposed to proceed with life now that my rock, my support, my protector—my mom—was gone? I attended church all my life and knew God was there for me, but as a fifteen-year-old when someone says, "It'll be all right; trust God," it doesn't help. Trusting God still doesn't bring my mom back. In hindsight, I wish I would have heeded those words of trusting fully in God. I know He would have met my heart's needs, but I was just so empty and lost.

Those first weeks and months without Mom at home were tough. Void is the only word that comes close to describing the experience. That was what our home felt like. That is what my life felt like. Life seemed like a void. Mom was gone. Becky went off to college that fall, which left my dad and me alone. The two of us learned valuable life lessons during that time as we tried to learn how to productively live again.

The dreams I had of Mom after she died were hard to handle. Two of them I knew were dreams and I didn't want to wake up. In the first, Mom was touching me again, and the love I felt through her touch I could feel in my dream. I remember waking up knowing the touch and love I had just felt was only a dream, and I lay on my bed and cried. In the second dream, Mom was telling me I was only dreaming and that when I woke up she wouldn't be there. I begged her to come back, but when my eyes opened, she was gone. Those dreams happened many years ago, but I have never forgotten them. I long to dream about her again, to feel her touch and love, to hear her voice again.

With Becky at college out of state, it was just my dad and me at the house. I did the house cleaning, laundry, and grocery shopping; cooked the meals; and packed the lunches. Needless to say, we ate a lot of premade pizzas, baked beans and hot dogs. Sometimes while I was standing at the kitchen sink, preparing the food, I looked out the window with such longing for my mom to walk around the garage, come into the kitchen, and make everything normal again. The tears flowed as I stared and prayed, longing for Mom to be back home with us. But I knew she would never be coming home again.

The death of a close loved one will undoubtedly leave scars in your life. Unfortunately, many people who lose someone close allow those scars to control them. God never meant for us to live under that weight of hopelessness. It is normal for scars to form in our lives when a loved one dies. Each of us grieves differently and for different lengths of time. Crying is okay. Honestly, crying helps your body, soul, and mind heal.

What you do with the scars of death is an important decision. The scars will never go away. In fact, I cry each time I have revised or reread this chapter. Although this event happened over half my lifetime ago, the scars are still real. They still affect me but they will not control me. I must allow those scars to heal. Scars are always with you, but you alone decide how they will heal.

The scars of my mother's death are difficult, even though she died twenty-five years ago. But because of those scars of death, I have been able to empathize and sympathize with people who have lost a loved one. I have been able to love them, help guide them in their time of loss, and do what I can to help them with their scars that do last a lifetime. Funerals are the hardest things for me to do as a pastor because the loss of a close family member is often so overwhelming. At each funeral, I battle the scars of death I have encountered in my lifetime.

Within the last decade, I have had to deal with those scars again as my father-in-law, Tim, bravely fought pancreatic cancer for over three years, a battle he lost at the age of fifty. He was three years older than my mother was when she died. I know what it is like to lose those I love. I know the pain is still real even after so many years have passed. I also know and believe that the strength and hope we can receive from God is strong enough to help us through the scars of death.

Mom had accepted Jesus into her heart and I know she is in Heaven with Him. She was a Christian and is now enjoying eternity free of pain because of her faith in Jesus. The same goes for Tim, as he loved the Lord with all his heart also.

I often use the following poem at funeral services. If you are experiencing deep scars from the death of a loved one, I trust that this will encourage and strengthen you and that you will allow God to carry you through the scars of death.

Footprints

(Author Unknown)

One night a man had a dream. He dreamed he was walking along the beach with the LORD. Across the sky flashed scenes from his life. For each scene he noticed two sets of footprints in the sand: one belonging to him, and the other to the LORD.

When the last scene of his life flashed before him, he looked back at the footprints in the sand. He noticed that many times along the path of his life there was only one set of footprints.

He also noticed that it happened at the very lowest and saddest times in his life. This really bothered him and he questioned the LORD about it:

"LORD, you said that once I decided to follow you, you'd walk with me all the way. But I have noticed that during the most troublesome times in my life, there is only one set of footprints. I don't understand why when I needed you most you would leave me."

The LORD replied:

"My son, my precious child, I love you and I would never leave you. During your times of trial and suffering, when you see only one set of footprints, it was then that I carried you."

CUSTOM SCARS & CUSTOM CARS

At this point in my life, I was completely in pieces, just like Dad's 1948 Ford Sedan during its earliest stages of customization. Dad tore that Sedan into pieces and laid them out, bare, exposed, dirty, and a mess. He eventually replaced them with pieces he found at swap meets and other outlets. You could say at this point that I related to his *Custom Car* when it was in pieces. After all, what could anyone do for a boy who lost his world?

Someone has probably brazenly told you to just gather the broken pieces of your life and keep going. I honestly don't think the pieces should just be gathered up randomly. They need to be examined and a plan needs to be laid out to put the custom pieces back together. When you are in as many pieces as I was, care and concern are needed to rebuild in a positive way.

My dad didn't tear this car apart to just have everything strewn all over the place (although sometimes the basement looked like that, but he knew, most of the time, where things were). Even though the car was in pieces, often all over the garage floor and shelves, he organized them with the purpose of building a complete *Custom Car* just the way he wanted.

The pieces of my life were laid out on the floor, as well, and needed to be reassembled by the Master Builder, the one who can shape a broken fifteen-year-old into the person he is to become. My life was like Dad's car parts, but God wasn't going to let those parts just sit there. The Master Builder started to put the pieces back where He wanted them to go, and healing and hope began to grow.

My customization hasn't stopped and it will continue until the day I die. I needed God to put the pieces of my custom life back together. I needed His master plan. Even today, as long as I continue to allow my heavenly "Father" to put my pieces together, I will embrace and use my *Custom Scars* for Him.

four

THE SCAR FOR LIFE

Life at home started to level off by the winter of 1993. We were all becoming more adjusted to life without Mom. Healing in various realms was slowly occurring within our family. Honestly, when something this tragic happens, the emotions and feelings can take years to heal. This healing wasn't suddenly evident and all wasn't perfect in the world, but my father really did desire to become the father he'd neglected to be when we were growing up. At the age of fifty-one, he was trying to change even when I didn't care about his changes.

Over the next few years, my father worked extremely hard at healing the relationships with his children. He took proactive steps to become a better father and a better man. It took a while, but I started to have hope that my dad was changing for the betterment of his family. One of the last things my mother challenged my father with was to find another wife and treat her the way a wife should be treated. He accepted that challenge but found that it was a larger task than he had in mind.

Before he could do what my mother requested, he had to have a change of heart, a change in actions, a change in communication, and a change in appreciation. Honestly, I don't know everything he did to facilitate these changes in his life, but I do know he allowed God to change him.

It was nearly a year since my mother died when odd events started to happen. I was sixteen now and my father started dating. He even bought a Cadillac in order to have his "ride" for the dates! I can't remember how many first dates he had (or second, for that matter), but he had far more dates than I did!

I wasn't opposed to my father finding another wife. The changes in Dad at this point were small but measurable. I knew it was going to be a difficult transition if Dad did remarry, but as a sixteen-year-old, I wasn't particularly fond of doing all the cooking, cleaning, laundry, and grocery shopping. Having someone else come in to help wasn't too bad of an idea.

Multiple times my father offered to take me and a "date" with him on his dates. He said that he would even cover the tab. Let me tell you that there are two things in this scenario that just didn't work. First, I never had a desire to go on a double date with my father, and second, I didn't have anyone to take on a date. (What teenage girl would even be willing to come under that scenario anyway?)

I was also that guy who was friends with many girls in high school but never had a girlfriend. Twice in high school I did attempt to start a relationship. One girl told me she would date me if my personality was different, and another girl told me if it didn't work out with this other guy, she would consider dating me. Maybe I should consider those emotional scars since I remember them so well. Either way, I wasn't part of the dating scene in high school, which also posed the question of whether someone would love such a scarred person.

(My dad's dating life was a unique time, and I am somewhat glad I can't remember a whole lot about that part of my life.)

My sister decided not to go back to college after her freshman year. So it was now the fall of 1994, and my sister found a job working at an assisted living facility about twenty-five miles from home. She lived at home and drove the distance each day to work.

With Becky returning home to live, the dynamics within our household changed again and the adjustment wasn't always pleasant. I was out late with friends many nights, sometimes until one or two in the morning, and Becky often stayed up and waited for me to get home. Dad never really gave me a curfew, as long as I kept doing the household chores and my schoolwork. My sister was concerned I was going to get into trouble and wanted to make sure I was safe. I told her to her face that I wanted nothing to do with her "parental" support. I got quite upset at her staying up and waiting for me, though in hindsight, her concern for my welfare and safety displayed her love for me. If all siblings cared for each other like Becky cared for me, our society would be a much better place to live.

In November 1994 my sister started dating a man seriously. He eventually became her husband, but that's down the road a bit. After my sister started to date, she spent a lot of time with Chris, her boyfriend, after work. I got along fine with Chris, as he worked for Dad occasionally.

So at this point, my sister was in a relationship, I was not in any, of course, and my dad was still alone. It wasn't until a friend of my dad encouraged him to call a widow he knew. Her name was Kathy DeMent and her husband had died of a brain aneurysm in 1990.

Kathy gave their mutual friend permission to give my dad her number. My father gave her a call and asked if she would be willing to go on a date with him. Thankfully she said yes and I didn't go on a double date with them that night. (Or any night)

Date night came and Dad brought Kathy to the house to meet the kids. I can't remember if Becky was home, but I know that I was. She saw a date marked on the wall calendar, June 25, as "Dad's Birthday," and asked "Who is 'Dad'?" I pointed at Dad and said, "It's Dad's!" Kathy proceeded to inform us that June 25 was her birthday too.

I stated earlier about my sharing a birthday with my grandfathers. Now my dad shares his birthday with my stepmom. What are the chances of that ever happening? This was a unique coincidence, but what makes it even odder is that my sister's and brother-in-law's birthdays are on the same day, too! The wheels in my head started turning. Did this mean I would marry someone whose birthday was on Valentine's Day? Only time would tell. . .

My dad and sister both got married in 1995. It was a difficult transition having someone come into the house where I grew up and then having my sister move out. During the month prior to and after his wedding to Kathy, Dad really worked hard to continue to mend the broken paths in the relationships with my sister and me. It was difficult for us all, but I am so glad I had an example of a man who can change for the glory of God and for the strength of his family. I was even the best man at Dad and Kathy's wedding.

After all the weddings happened and the new normal started to develop, it was now my senior year of high school. Our household consisted of my father, Kathy, and me. Kathy and her late husband had three other children who were married and had children of their own by the time my dad and Kathy were married, so I was the lone child in the house. I was glad I didn't have to do all the cooking, cleaning, and laundry anymore. I was glad Dad had found someone to share his life with too.

For those who have lived in a blended family, you know it can be difficult at times. When a family blends together, all the good and the bad come along with it. The dynamics of holidays and even family traditions change when two families combine. Adjustments and compromise are part of the blending process. It will never be the "same" as it was before the loss of a parent, but it isn't meant to be. The blending of families is a new chapter, and the pen is in the family members hands.

My senior year of high school was fantastic. I had great friends, many good times, and seemed to be in good health. It was quite a different experience from my younger years of school with the teasing and torments. My senior year was filled with so many good times of being with friends around campfires, playing pool, going to the arcade, and hiking. I still keep in contact with many of those friends today.

After graduation, I started doing some carpentry work for a neighbor. He was building a gazebo for his daughter's wedding later that summer. I knew some things about heavy equipment from working with Dad, but my carpentry skills were next to nothing. That inexperience bore its fruit while I was using a table saw one afternoon. I was cutting slender strips of wood to be breathing strips for the gazebo roof. I pulled a piece of wood through the saw, which is a no-no, and the saw blade pulled the piece of wood out of my hand. I thought the wood was the only casualty, but my hand also hit the saw blade. It happened so fast. I looked down at my hand and the end of my right index finger was gone. The saw blade went right through the top knuckle. The top third of my finger was completely gone and the search began to try to find it.

Being in a smaller community, I was able to be taken to a surgeon whose sons I attended high school with. Dr. Smith got me in pronto, considered sewing my finger back on, which one of my friends found fifteen feet away from the saw, but with Marfan syndrome, he didn't want to add a risk of infection if the fingertip didn't reconnect. He thought that even without the end of my finger, it would still be as long as everyone else's. So Dr. Smith proceeded to sew the end of my finger closed, and in less than an hour we headed home.

Since the finger was not reattached, we kept the cut-off end in a sandwich bag in the freezer. I asked people who stopped by the house if they wanted to see it. My finger was only safe in the freezer for a few months because one day it ended up getting stuck to my dad's ice pack and put in his lunch. It went to work with him that day and hasn't been seen since. Cutting the end of my finger off slowed my summer down because I was incapacitated for nearly two months.

I didn't want to go to college that fall like most of my friends. My dream was to secure a job as a disc jockey. (Considering radio as a profession started when I was part of a radio project in ninth grade, and my teacher, Mr. Fedei, encouraged me to consider radio as a career. That little encouragement from my teacher was all I needed. The power of positive words can change someone's life.) I quickly found out that radio isn't the easiest career to jump into right out of high school when you have no experience or connections. I applied to all the local radio stations within thirty miles but didn't get a single call back.

During that fall I stayed home and tried to figure out what to do with my life. The one thing I needed to do was see my cardiologist for my yearly visit, the results of which I assumed would be the same as the year before. I figured that my aortic measurements would be fine. Apparently my activities over that past year, which included three-on-three basketball tournaments, many rollercoaster rides, and even bungee jumping, had caused the doctors to find something of concern during this visit.

My cardiologist informed me that my aortic valve needed to be replaced. So he referred me to a surgeon, who in turn described to me what was happening to my aortic valve and root. Dr. Magovern, the surgeon, told me to imagine that my aorta is the size of a garden hose and the valve going into my heart is the size of the end of the garden hose that I would twist onto the water supply. Then he told me to imagine a pear on the end of the hose, the big end of the pear being the valve, and the smaller end being the size of the aorta coming from the valve. That was how large my aortic valve and root had become over the course of a year.

Dr. Magovern scheduled me for open-heart surgery the first week in January 1997 at Allegheny General Hospital in Pittsburgh. With that diagnosis I kept my physical activity to a minimum so my valve wouldn't enlarge anymore. I was aware of the physical stresses I had put on my valve throughout the previous year and knew which activities I needed to rein back. More than my initial fears from

38

when I was twelve, I now had a literal feeling that my aorta could burst. The possibility was all too real and the outcome of a tear could be fatal.

Looking back it was a blessing that I had cut my finger off in June, as the carpentry work was physically demanding. I believe that was God's preventative care and concern for my life when I didn't even realize it. Matthew 10:29-30 says that God is concerned when even one sparrow falls to the ground, so how much more is He concerned for my life and yours? Because of my limited carpentry skills and the accident, I limited the wear on my aorta that summer.

Six weeks before my open-heart surgery, my surgeon wanted me to donate my own blood to help eliminate the risk of blood transfusion problems. Each week I drove forty miles to the blood donation center where nurses would alternate arms, and by the end of this process, my arms were sore and my veins were broken down. During this period, my surgery had also been postponed a week, which caused one of my units of blood to expire. I tried to give for a seventh week, but the nurse could only take half a unit because my veins had deteriorated. I was ready to be done with this whole routine anyhow.

After I'd donated all the blood I was capable of, the time had finally come for the surgeon to replace my aortic valve and root. My replacement actually came from a cadaver and was called a homograph. The incredible thing with a homograph is that my body would not reject it. This procedure was relatively new, and the results had all been very encouraging. Plus, I didn't have to be on a blood thinner, unlike if I'd had an artificial heart valve. All positive things since I was so young.

My recovery time was very quick due to my age, and I was in no need of advanced heart care. Typically people in the heart wing of a hospital are three to four times my age and on special diets and restrictions. It was unique for the nursing staff to have an eighteen-year-old patient motivated to get out.

The nursing staff at the hospital treated me with incredible kindness. Throughout the years, I have found that a supportive family and a supportive medical staff at my side sped up recovery time exponentially. The surgery was a complete success, and I was in the hospital less than a week with my parents always making sure I was doing well. I made it home with my first of many literal scars on my body, the scar of open-heart surgery . . . right down the middle of my chest! Boy, did I have a story to tell now! Not every eighteen-year-old has had open heart surgery. I was glad it was over and Dr. Magovern was quite pleased with the results of the procedure.

Other than bike wrecks and a finger being sawed off, I am now starting to accumulate some unique *Custom Scars* related to Marfan syndrome. Through God's grace, however, I survived the diagnosis of this genetic condition, the death of my mother, and now open-heart surgery. Those days were not easy, but they were again more building blocks of who I would become as a man.

Less than three weeks after the surgery, I left for Kentucky to start a college degree in religion and communications. I only agreed to attend if I would be able to work at the radio station associated with the college. So my parents packed me up and we headed to Kentucky Mountain Bible College, where my sister and brother-in-law were currently living. Chris was taking classes for his calling in pastoral ministry.

The college was small, but I was fine with that. All I cared about was gaining experience at the radio station. I'll never forget that first day of class in January 1997. I got up for breakfast and then walked over to the chapel. It wasn't long after I sat down for my first chapel experience that I began feeling ill. So I excused myself, made it outside quick, and got sick. What a way to start my college life, but my advisor and still good friend, Dr. John Neihof, came outside to see what he could do to help me. He took me to get a drink of water and we sat down for a while. He has been looking out for me and loving me ever since the first day I walked onto that campus.

During my first semester of college I took a light college load of eight credit hours. I also started to work at the radio station, WMTC, which was a dream come true. I regained much of my strength from the surgery, and I was steadily getting my feet back under me.

As that first semester of college was coming to a close, I had gradually made it back to my pre-surgery activity level. I felt really good and was so glad that my chest/sternum wasn't sore anymore. I then decided that since it had been three months since I'd last sneezed, that I could again allow myself to. Those who have had open-heart surgery know that sneezing doesn't feel the best; therefore, I didn't sneeze for months. Trust me, it can be done, but it wasn't easy.

Although I was doing considerably better, some folks around me saw a slow regression in my stamina throughout the month of May. It wasn't terribly evident, as even I didn't notice a change. Something was happening inside my body as a result of the surgery in January. Not until the semester ended and I went back to Pennsylvania for a couple of weeks, with a doctor's appointment scheduled, did the doctor discover something that would lead to a miracle.

As I alluded to, I am a pretty thin guy. When I went back to Pennsylvania this time, I weighed five pounds more than my pre-surgery weight. I was so happy to be able to see Dr. Magovern and share my progress and weight gain with him. That was supposed to be an indicator of improvement, right?

When we arrived at the hospital, the doctors performed the normal electrocardiogram (EKG) and echocardiogram and easily saw fluid around my heart. "What do you mean 'fluid' around my heart?" I wondered, not understanding how I could have fluid there. The doctors then told me that when they perform open-heart surgery, they cut through the pericardium to get to the heart. The pericardium is the membrane, or bag, that holds a person's heart where it is supposed to be. This was all news to me, but if you are reading this, you have a pericardium too.

Apparently when they cut through my pericardium to access my heart, the incision didn't heal properly and it was leaking fluid inside itself. This fluid had been building up around my heart over the course of the last four to five months. After Dr. Magovern saw the fluid, he said we needed to stay at the hospital so they could remove it immediately. Straight from his office we headed to surgery so a different surgeon could tap off the fluid from around my heart. This is when the miracle happened.

They used a local anesthetic to numb the area below my sternum and inserted a needle under my ribs (which didn't feel very good), that went the whole way up to my pericardium and punctured it. Then the surgeon ran a tube through that needle and inside my pericardium. That tube then went up around my heart. I could feel the tube being pushed inside me. It didn't hurt but it was a rather uncomfortable experience.

The surgeon used equipment (x-ray stuff) so he could see what he was doing inside me. I watched the entire procedure, as well, while I was lying on the table, feeling every inch of that needle and tube.

Once the tube was in place around my heart, the surgeon began to extract the fluid. I was comfortable having the procedure done in such a prompt fashion because the surgeon was one of the best and had decades of experience. He was a pioneer in this procedure and had performed taps like this on thousands of others. He thought mine was going to be a normal fluid tap until the procedure continued.

As the draining took longer and longer, a look of surprise came over the faces of those in the room, as the surgeon just kept removing more and more fluid from my pericardium. He and the others knew there was a substantial amount but never expected this much.

The surgeon was draining the fluid into a container sitting on my chest, which was filling up quickly -- one liter of fluid, two liters of fluid. The surgeon didn't quite reach three liters when he said it was all out. The tube and needle were removed. Relieved the procedure was complete, I headed back to a hospital room for the night.

The pressure of fluid that had accumulated around my heart should have been greater than its beating capacity. Medically and logically, my heart shouldn't have been able to keep going. After the surgeon saw the amount of fluid, which would have weighed more than six pounds, he was perplexed. He told my parents that he had never taken that much fluid out of a living person. They told him it was a miracle and God still had plans for my life. Jeremiah 29:11 speaks of this. "For I know the plans I have for you," declares the LORD, "plans to

God simply wasn't finished with me yet.

prosper you and not to harm you, plans to give you hope and a future." Astonished at what had just occurred, the doctor was speechless at this medical miracle. God simply wasn't finished with me yet.

Relieved that this experience was behind me, we headed home the following day. That next week I traveled back to Kentucky Mountain Bible College to work for the summer, not realizing the significance of what had occurred. At the end of the summer the surgeon needed to repeat the procedure, but this time he only took out ten ounces of fluid. Since then, I have had no more pericardial effusions for which I am very thankful.

That first year after open-heart surgery was another growing experience for me. I began thinking about if and how these scars would affect my future. While I could cover the outward scars to hide them from the world, I saw them every day. Would I find someone to love me even though I was not "normal"? Would this scar down my chest deter a woman from accepting me?

As a nineteen-year-old, I wondered what my life would be like. I just wanted things to settle down and be normal. At that point, however, I had to ask myself, "What is normal?" The answer is, "I *am* normal!" Yes. Are you normal? Yes. We are all normal because we are exactly who God made us to be regardless of the visible or invisible scars that we carry.

These first scars of surgery were the start of a journey of compassion and hope for those with their own *Custom Scars*. The scars that come into our lives that we have no control over are ours for a reason. We have to accept and use them to help others with their *Custom Scars*. You can find hope in the midst of your pain. Healing is available. Psalm 121:2 is a verse you can cling to when battling the scars of life. "My help comes from the LORD, the Maker of heaven and earth." The God who created everything is willing to help you and He loves you. You can take incredible hope in those amazing facts.

CUSTOM SCARS & CUSTOM CARS

Years before my father even started building his 1948 Ford, he was planning the build and customizations. He had a good idea what he wanted it to look like and run like. When I was sixteen, he bought a 1969 Chevelle that had a 350 engine in it so he could put that engine into the 1948 Ford which he wouldn't begin building until years later. That Chevelle ended up being my first car to try to restore. I tore some of it apart, sandblasted the front end, but then just parked it. Restoring that car was too big of a project for a teenager who really didn't have any income to invest.

Dad bought that Chevelle for one thing only, its engine. So he pulled that 350 out and tucked it aside until the day he began his *Custom Car*. Dad desired to have a different engine in his car, a custom engine. This first surgery on my heart valve was the first step in my custom engine, the custom pieces that would be surgically used to keep my engine going.

As people look at Dad's *Custom Car* and its engine, he doesn't get negative comments but compliments about its uniqueness, worth, and value. That's exactly how God wants us to view our own *Custom Scars*. My engine, my heart valve, was replaced and my Master Builder is thrilled at the customization. My value hasn't decreased or increased because of my valve. My value remains the same to God. I am priceless, special, and loved, even after I had a piece of my engine replaced.

No matter what may have been replaced or fixed in your life, God will always love you. God desires the customizations in your life to be used for good. What you do with your life is your choice, but God is willing and able to help you with your *Custom Scars*.

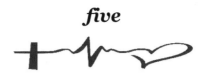

five

BECOMING SOMETHING WITH THESE SCARS

My first semester of college I just wanted to get away from home and work at a radio station. I figured I could go to Bible College and just go through the "Christian" motions like I had throughout high school. I accomplished that my first semester, but as I started my first full year of college, I knew I couldn't be fully satisfied with life by trying to do things in my own strength or going through the religious motions. I knew I needed strength and encouragement from more than just my family, friends, and professors.

I had gone to church all my life and went to a Christian school from grades K-12, but I truly hadn't given my life's dreams, goals, and my all to God to use as He desired. During that semester of my first full year at college, I submitted my all to the Lord and made a solid commitment to Him during a chapel service in Myers Chapel. At an altar of prayer, I surrendered to do what He wanted me to do and go where He wanted me to go. This was an important step in my growth as a Christian, but I always assumed Christian radio would be a significant part of that journey.

After I let God take control of my life, I had a greater motivation to excel in my schoolwork. I was not an honor-roll student in high school, but in college I started to care about my academics. I didn't get all As, but I never received a grade lower than a B-. I also worked twenty to twenty-five hours a week at the campus radio station. Regardless of Marfan syndrome, I worked hard and had a deep desire to succeed. I was going to work as hard as I was able to and not get caught up in the fact that I had some limitations.

During this time of my life, I remembered back to what my mother told me after I was initially diagnosed with Marfan syndrome. She said pointing at her head, "Stephen, you wouldn't be able to make a living using your physical strength, so you'll need to use your brain." Nowadays, that's scary to think about since all my medical procedures have hindered my mental capacities, but God's grace is enough even in my forgetful times. When my memories are gray, I often give a disclaimer that my forgetfulness is a result of the numerous surgeries in my life. I have heeded my mother's advice and am using my mind to the best of its abilities.

The summer after my full freshman year of college, I traveled with the college drama team, which consisted of two guys and two girls. Dave, Amy, Sara, and I traveled hundreds of miles together to youth camps across the eastern part of the United States. I have been blessed with friends who never even batted an eye because of my scars. In fact, Dave is still one of my best friends. He never labeled me or treated me any different from anyone else. He is a friend in the truest form. So often folks who are "different" are excluded and outcast, but we all need friends and I'm so glad I have a friend in Dave.

I was now realizing more and more how God could use the scars in my life to encourage and help others! How my scars can help others have hope.

That summer of ministry was one of the greatest summers of my life. We traveled to eight summer camps to perform dramas, lead singing, and counsel kids. I had many opportunities to share my life story. I connected with kids who had suffered the loss of a loved one or who had a physical challenge, whether visible or hidden. I was now realizing more and more how God could use the scars in my life to encourage and help others! How my scars can help others have hope. Philippians 2:13 states, "For it is God who works in you to will and to act according to his good purpose." The way God created me wasn't a mistake, and God's plans for my life were becoming clearer.

At one of the camps, I met a teenage boy who had so much hurt in his family life and had recently lost a parent. I was able to share and encourage this young man at a time when his scars were still so real and painful. A bond formed between us. After that week was over and the kids were heading home, he ran up to me with a gift. He was wearing a necklace that had a little gecko on it, and he gave it to me so I wouldn't forget him. I gave him a bracelet and he hugged me. Then he walked to the vehicle that took him home and I haven't seen him since.

I still have that necklace. My oldest daughter sometimes wears it. I told her the story behind the necklace and stressed that she had better not lose it!

The drama team had many wonderful experiences that summer as a group, along with personal, life-changing ones. In fact, two experiences forever changed my life. They happened in different weeks and in two different states.

One of those experiences happened while I was ministering for two weeks at a camp in Danville, Virginia. Each evening we had a church service for the campers. Although many of them were spiritually helped, I believe this particular service was what set me fully on the path I am walking today.

Maybe you have attended a church service or camp meeting where the congregation sings a closing chorus over and over. The goal is to encourage people to get right with God at an altar if the Lord had spoken to them during the service. At the close of one of those evening services the Lord was leading me to go forward, but I fought with the Lord about going up to that altar. I just wanted the service to end so I didn't need to respond, but that chorus just kept being sung! I didn't want to go forward because I knew what God was asking me to do. He was telling me I needed to let go of my desire to work in the radio profession. I sat in that pew literally fighting God, grabbing hold of the pew in front of me, resolutely not going to that altar.

I LOVE WORKING IN RADIO! I'm screaming in my head and my heart. Even though I had already told God I was His to use, I still figured He would use me in the field of Christian radio. So why did He want me to go forward? *This song is never going to end!* I kept saying to myself. *Why are we still singing the same stupid chorus! Please stop!*

After what seemed like an eternity, a camp counselor from Asbury College approached me and asked if I needed to go to the altar for prayer. Knowing that God had something in mind for me at that altar, I let go of the pew in front of me, blood now circulating past my white knuckles, and made my way to the altar.

Honestly, I was afraid God was going to call me to be a pastor. I didn't want to be a pastor! Even as I was at the altar, I knew God had a plan for my life, but was everything, including my life's vocation, going to change? What did God want from me, or even with me, at this altar? I already told Him that He could use me however He wanted, but God wasn't interested in my talk. He wanted me to fully surrender my all to Him.

After a good twenty minutes of internal wrestling, God helped me realize that all He was asking me to do was be willing to give up radio to Him. That was all. He just wanted me to take my hands off and allow Him to do the guiding and directing. At that moment, I took my hands off the direction I had set for my life and submitted fully to whatever path God desired for me. As I mentioned before, Jeremiah 29:11 speaks of God's plans of hope and a future. Plans of prosperity and not harm. All God wanted from me was to give it <u>all</u> to Him.

Although I relinquished my control of working in radio that night, God wasn't finished with me in that field. He just needed me to take my hands off it so He could direct me on another path in the future if that was His will. He wanted to make sure I was following His plan and not my plan for my life.

That experience was a milestone, a stake in the ground, and a monumental point in my life. I have never been the same since I submitted my all to the direction of God. That evening I surrendered everything, including the scars from my past and the scars of my future, to the One who unconditionally loves my *Custom Scars*.

> **That evening I surrendered everything, including the scars from my past and the scars of my future, to the One who unconditionally loves my Custom Scars.**

The second event occurred in my home state of Pennsylvania. It was actually the last day of the last camp of the summer. I wasn't feeling the best that day because my friend, Dave, had dropped me on my head a couple of days prior. This is going to sound crazy, but the kids at the camp thought dog piles (tackling a person and then piling on top of him or her) were a great idea. Unfortunately, Dave came up behind me, put his arms around me to pin my arms to my side, and picked me up. The problem was he picked me up too low on my body and too high off the ground, and because of the top-heavy weight, we fell forward. I landed with all my weight and his weight on my head, as it rolled under me.

I honestly thought my neck broke; I heard multiple cracks and couldn't move my arms or legs. After a few minutes and some tingling, however, feeling did come back. I had some vertebrae out of place that the chiropractor cracked back into their proper positions the following week.

So during this final service on Sunday morning the congregation took communion. Communion is when grape juice and bread are used to symbolize the broken body and spilled blood of Jesus. It is an important sacrament for Christians. When the bread and grape juice were distributed, the leader of the camp, Barry Weyant, shared some Scripture pertaining to the sacrament of communion. As he spoke, an incredible sense of the presence of God came over me in that tabernacle. I was sitting by myself, with no one by me or near me, and I heard the audible voice of God speaking to me. Hopefully you don't think I am crazy, a thought that did cross my mind at the time. There I was, a twenty-year-old finishing up a summer of affecting people's lives, and God chose to speak to me in a real audible way. I heard the clear voice of God say He was going to take care of me and everything would be all right.

I was startled because I am not talking about a warm fuzzy feeling or hearing something internally; it was an audible voice to me. When I looked around and saw no one near me, I knew it was God speaking.

I began to weep in absolute awe that God would care for a scarred person like me. Those words have resonated within me ever since, and those two experiences changed my life.

As I continued my college life, I made many good choices along with some pretty bad ones. God always remained faithful even when I took a detour from His direction. He always sought me when I wasn't walking with Him as I should have been. I also had great teachers and classmates who helped me stay on the right track.

Even as a college student, I knew life outside of college would hold a unique set of challenges for me. As I made my way closer to my senior year, I became more keenly aware of my need for absolute surrender to the direction of God. Also, God knew I needed someone to walk beside me throughout the lifelong journey I was about to embark on after graduation. I knew God loved me, *Custom Scars* and all, but could a girl ever love such an emotionally and physically scarred person?

CUSTOM SCARS & CUSTOM CARS

During my college years, some significant pieces of my life were coming together. Just like my dad working on his 1948 Ford Sedan, cleaning up the parts and starting to assemble the car, God was significantly putting the broken pieces of my life together. Dad's *Custom Car* was taking shape the way he desired it to be. In the same way, God had given me these two life-changing experiences to build me the way He wanted me to be.

God's design for our lives is never wrong or faulty. You may question this because of all the sickness and evil in the world, or maybe because of the sickness and suffering you are personally experiencing. I can understand these types of questions because life can be really tough. Some of you have had scars in your life that I cannot even comprehend. Such pains will always be part of this world. I am truly thankful that God has given us a way through His Son, Jesus, to not be bound by these scars but to allow Him to use them for His glory and have hope in Him.

Dad's custom 1948 Ford was looking better, but he still had a long way to go. Since I had given my all to the Lord, things were looking better for me, but I also had a long way to go and a long way to grow.

six

LOVED WITH SCARS

As I have said, my dating life in high school was pretty much non-existent. In fact, I only held a girl's hand once during those years (she willingly held my hand), but I had no idea what to do from that point! I was so scared that I didn't talk to her for days because I didn't know what to do or say. This became really awkward because our lockers were right next to each other. I liked holding this girl's hand but apparently I needed some communication follow-up. Oops.

In college I liked a few girls and even dated one seriously (whose birthday was the same as mine) before the young woman who became my wife arrived on campus. I was a junior and she was an incoming freshman. I would graduate in two years with my bachelor's degree and many of the new girls would graduate that same year with their associate's degrees, so that was the group to focus on, right? When Amanda arrived on campus, I was actually really interested in another girl, but that fell apart during the second semester of my junior year.

Amanda and I started our courtship at the end of my junior year and Amanda's freshman year. Neither of us desired to just date, but to purposely head down a path that could lead toward marriage. That summer I spent six weeks in Haiti doing my internship at a Christian mission radio station, 4VEH, which is the work of One Mission Society (OMS). Earlier that year in college, an OMS representative shared about internship opportunities overseas and I felt I should pursue those opportunities. All the finances and paperwork came through without a problem, and that June I headed for Haiti.

During those weeks of being separated from Amanda our courtship grew stronger. Emails were sent regularly, and during our separation we both felt fairly confident that we were progressing toward marriage.

After I arrived home from Haiti and saw her again, I was even more confident that she was the one. Surprisingly, her mother knew the first day her parents met me that "this boy is going to marry our daughter."

We became engaged during the first semester of my senior year and planned to marry that summer. I couldn't believe someone would ever love me with all these scars! I was so different in appearance, my body scarred from surgery, that I couldn't understand how someone could love me this way. She didn't even mind that I was more than a foot taller than she was!

Remember when I said when I was in high school that a girl actually told me if I had a different personality she would consider dating me? Now someone was willing to spend the rest of her life with me and she liked my personality. She laughed at my jokes, too! This girl really loved me.

As Amanda and I drew closer, I was willing to open up about the scars in my life. Even today I share about these scars and their effects on me. She has never stopped accepting me regardless of my scars. During our premarital counseling sessions, we learned so much more about each other. Those sessions were invaluable in building a solid marriage foundation. One of our college professors, Rev. Tom Lorimer, counseled us and helped officiate our wedding. His concern for our marriage remains evident today as he sends us an anniversary card each year.

I made it clear throughout our courtship and engagement that my health concerns are a daily part of my life and explained how they could affect our family. I had already had one surgery and didn't know if another one would be necessary. How would she handle that stress? Would she still love me despite more scars? What types of scars would she have to live through being married to me? What about raising a family?

During our premarital counseling sessions, we discussed family planning. This is something people with Marfan syndrome need to be aware of. Since Marfan syndrome is genetic, our children would have a 50% chance of being diagnosed with the condition. I knew what living with Marfan syndrome meant, but at the time, we didn't know how Marfans would eventually affect our children. We did know that we would love and care for our children without reserve, whether they had Marfan syndrome or not. Amanda and I felt the same as the Psalmist did in Psalm 33:22, "May your unfailing love rest upon us, O LORD, even as we put our hope in you."

Our hope was in the Lord and it didn't matter to us if all, some, or none of our future children had Marfan syndrome. We believe every life God creates is special, and we would be blessed to have the opportunity to raise children regardless of any physical limitations.

We can have so many questions about life and so often the answers only come through living. My final semester of college I attended Focus on the Family's Institute in Colorado Springs for a fairly extensive training on family, worldview, church, and moral issues. During this time away, God directed me to the next steps I was to take in my life.

Being more than twelve hundred miles away from Amanda made planning a wedding quite difficult. More importantly, she and I needed to know what we were to do after graduation. I had three opportunities to consider: 1) working at a local Pennsylvania Christian radio station, 2) working in Colorado, or 3) becoming a missionary and moving to Papua New Guinea.

I earnestly desired to do what God wanted. Remember the altar experience in Virginia? One evening in Colorado after I had read my Bible and then listened to the testimony of a man named David Ring, God clearly impressed on my heart that after graduation and marriage, Amanda and I were to go to Papua New Guinea.

The Scripture passage I read that day was from Matthew 28, the Great Commission that Jesus gave to His disciples. He told them to go into all the world and preach the Gospel. I thought about it a little. The Christian radio station in Pennsylvania and the ministries in Colorado would have plenty of applicants, but how many people would be willing to travel around the world to share Jesus via Christian radio?

Then there was the testimony of David Ring, a man with cerebral palsy, who challenges his hearers with a message that God has called him to preach despite his *Custom Scars*. In essence he asks, "So what are you doing with your life for Jesus?"

After reading Matthew 28 and listening to the testimony of David Ring, I immediately knew where God was leading. I called

Amanda and told her our journey as a married couple would take us to Papua New Guinea (PNG).

We married two weeks after graduating from college in 2001. Guess who the best man at my wedding was—my father. I didn't have him as the best man merely to reciprocate for me being the best man at his. My father was my best man because over the course of those last six or seven years, he allowed God to change him from the inside out. He did what my mother had challenged him to do. He changed for his new wife and his children. I could now look at my father and say, "I want to be like my dad." One's age doesn't matter to God when it comes to change. He will guide and direct anyone at any age at any time who is willing to obey.

Promptly after we were married, we started working and preparing for our lives in PNG. The first order of business was to raise financial support. We didn't have much time, as the radio equipment was going to arrive in PNG by the end of the year. That meant we had six months to raise enough support for us to live overseas for two years! A big task, but God always provides when we allow Him to lead.

Before we left the States, I also had to schedule my yearly checkup. In 2001, my doctor moved from Pittsburgh to Philadelphia, and we had an appointment set for September 12, 2001. So we headed to Philly on the afternoon of September 11.

Unfortunately, my doctor was in California on 9/11, and since all flights were grounded, he was stuck there. So we met with someone else in the department to review my echo to make sure all was fine with my valve and aorta. He asked us some general questions and we gave him our general answers. He told us the condition of my aorta looked stable. I then asked him whether I should be aware of anything as I traveled to Papua New Guinea. I will never forget his answer.

He just flat out said that we were stupid for traveling, and for us to go there was a foolish decision. Whoa! Was this his bedside manner? He belittled our decision and we left feeling harshly judged. Was he this condemning to all his patients he didn't agree with? Although I liked my regular doctor, we were not about to go back to this office ever again.

(Over the years I have had the opportunity to speak to various groups of medical students about Marfan syndrome. I often relay this story to make them aware that this type of treatment will effectively push patients away. They may not understand their patients' decisions, but belittling them is never appropriate. Providing clear medical advice and recommendations are fine, but a medical provider should never talk down to a patient. This associate didn't understand the spiritual aspect and the calling to missions.)

We proceeded with our plans to fly to PNG two days after Christmas because as Jesus stated in Matthew 19:26, "with God all things are possible."

Although we had spoken at only eight churches before we left, we had enough financial support because of the generosity of our family and church friends. I should add that Amanda was five months pregnant at the time. It may not have been our plans, but we were so thankful for God's plans.

In Papua New Guinea we helped start the first station in the PNG Christian Broadcasting Network: Wantok Radio Light. We experienced so many wonderful things there. God provided staff, funding, and, of course, He changed people's lives through Christian radio. We had so many great friends and supporters.

When our oldest, Michaela, was born, the people in PNG embraced her as one of their own. Many of the nationals were surprised to learn we intended for Michaela be born there because missionaries often traveled to Australia or back to the United States to give birth. But we found a nice private hospital operated by a midwife from New Zealand. She was wonderful, as were the locally trained staff.

When Amanda went into labor, the midwife was in New Zealand because her husband was having a heart procedure performed. So her trained staff of midwives walked us through the birth process of our first child. We had four midwives all wanting to be part of the birth of our daughter. Facilities were much different than those in the States when our other four children were born, but the PNG staff loved and took care of us. Michaela was born without issue in Papua New Guinea that May.

I was twenty-four years old and Amanda was just twenty-one. We were so young, but God knew the perfect plan for us and the perfect child to bless us with.

We experienced so many changes that year in PNG. We moved three times to find a nice location away from the station so we could have more personal space. The station was originally located in a three-bedroom apartment; we slept in one bedroom and the on-air and production rooms occupied the other two bedrooms. We used a communal kitchen and living room as people worked full-time in the apartment in which we lived. I learned how to drive on the opposite side of the road, tried to learn a little Pidgin English, and played basketball in a Filipino basketball league.

After that first busy year, we traveled back to the United States around Christmas to visit family and friends and, of course, have my yearly checkup. I started with a new cardiologist named Dr. Yvonne Maher. We stayed with her for more than a decade until she retired in 2015.

All seemed to go fine until the day of the appointment. With Marfan syndrome it is not only physical stress, like running or weight lifting, that can cause problems with the aorta, but also just intense life stress, and living overseas brought plenty of it. Most of it was good stress, such as having our first child in another country, but stress nonetheless. Playing in that basketball league may not have been the best idea though. At any rate, when I had my echo done, the doctor found an abdominal aortic aneurysm, or AAA.

My doctor warned us that if I was flying and my aneurysm would burst that my chance of survival would be next to nothing. So with a heavy heart, we had to inform the mission board that I had to step down from my position. Our daughter was only seven months old, many of our belongings were still over in PNG, and I was not allowed to fly back to retrieve them.

Amanda and my stepmom, Kathy, flew over to pack up our belongings and ship the rest back to the States. During our absence to the States, someone broke into our home in PNG and stole some of our belongings. Nothing of significant value, but my favorite ball cap was taken, which was actually the most difficult thing to lose. It was a fitted hat with the Nike logo on the front. I sure hope whoever has it now still enjoys it after all these years and it brings them as much joy as it did me.

They only spent a few days in Papua New Guinea to pack up the house, close our banking account, and say goodbye. They ended up cutting their trip short to rush back home, as I had experienced some peculiar chest pains and landed in the hospital. I was never able to say goodbye to my PNG friends, but I believe that someday I will have the opportunity to.

I wouldn't trade a minute of the time we had in PNG even if it meant not having this pending surgery. It was exactly where God wanted us to be for that year. Even though our plans were for two years, God knew what was best. I praise God for the one year He gave me in PNG to invest my life into that station.

We had so much support from EBM International, New Life Radio, HCJB, and the Papua New Guinea Bible Church. Many other national and international groups also contributed and supported this fantastic radio outreach to PNG. During that year I truly became a man in so many ways.

(The ministry has grown so much since it began in that three-bedroom apartment. The radio station is still effectively broadcasting Christian programming over the entire nation via shortwave radio and nearly thirty FM signals. The one thing that saddens me is that I will not be able to see the station manager, Pawa Warena, again until I reach heaven, as he has already passed into eternity. He was a great man who lived by faith. He loved his wife and his children so dearly, and I will never forget his love for me, my family, the station, his country, and his Savior.)

This was Amanda's first time being with me for a health procedure and I didn't know how she was going to react. Stories had been told, but when push came to shove, I didn't know how she was going to handle it. I was now twenty-five and Amanda was twenty-two, and this surgery wasn't as easy as open heart.

This aneurysm was on the other side of the arch of my aorta, and because of its size, we needed to schedule the surgery fairly quickly. The surgeon needed to replace the top half of my descending abdominal aorta with an artificial piece. The surgeon couldn't access the aneurysm through the middle of my chest as in open heart; instead, he needed to enter through the side.

Surgery was in January 2003. The surgeon told me it was going to be invasive, but I couldn't fathom the pain until it was done. The incision starts beside my belly button and goes all the way up and around my left side, under my left arm, and up to my left shoulder blade. The scar is over two feet long. The doctor also had to remove one of my ribs on my left side to access the area. That rib was just left out and the surgeon pulled the rib above and below closer to where the now-void space was located, to compensate for its removal.

The pain during recovery was excruciating. I continually prayed for the pain to decrease as my pain levels seemed unbearable. I don't know how Amanda was able to bear the burden of caring for our family while I was out of commission, except that she received her strength from the Lord. Just as we are instructed in 1 Peter 5:7, Amanda put all of her cares and anxiety on Jesus because she knew that He cared for her.

During this time I found out what it was like to experience unconditional love from my wife. She was beside me at the hospital practically every day and night. She didn't care if I now had a scar around most of my left side or that multiple tubes were coming out of my body. She was right there beside me.

At the beginning of my recovery period in the hospital, I told Amanda it was just too hard and hurt too much. I wanted to give up. I cannot adequately describe the physical pain, but I truly felt like my life was finished. The pain was all-engulfing. The will to fight was all but gone. I felt as if all hope was lost.

"What about me?" asked Amanda. "What about Michaela?" I told her they would be better off without me because my body was weak, and I didn't know how I would be able to provide for our family's needs. I told her there were other men she could marry who wouldn't have the issues I had and I just needed to die. She reassured me that she, Michaela, and the rest of my family did need me and that my life was valuable and worth fighting for.

Still not convinced, I was lying in bed with music playing in the background. Music had helped bring hope to me in the past. I heard a song titled, "It Is Well." The author of that song wrote it while on a ship crossing the Atlantic Ocean. He wrote it over the spot where his four daughters had perished at sea roughly two weeks prior. If the author, Horatio Spafford, could pen the words "It Is Well" with my (his) soul after such a loss, then by God's grace and strength it could be well with my soul even after such a traumatic surgery. The lyrics penetrated my heart and soul.

When peace, like a river, attendeth my way,
When sorrows like sea billows roll;
Whatever my lot, Thou hast taught me to say,
It is well, it is well with my soul.

Though Satan should buffet, tho' trials should come,
Let this blest assurance control,
That Christ has regarded my helpless estate,
And hath shed His own blood for my soul.

My sin – oh, the bliss of this glorious tho't
My sin – not in part, but the whole
Is nailed to the cross and I bear it no more,
Praise the Lord, praise the Lord, O my soul!

And, Lord, haste the day when the faith shall be sight,
The clouds be rolled back as a scroll,
The trump shall resound and the Lord shall descend,
"Even so" – it is well with my soul.

The chorus repeats the words "It is well with my soul." After listening to that song, with tears flowing down my face, I knew God would take care of me and my family. My life had been spared again and "It Is Well" with my soul.

With this surgery I had numerous chest tubes. If you have ever had tubes in your chest, you know they are uncomfortable and feel great when they are out, but the removal process isn't typically enjoyable. I hate chest tubes!

The surgeon's assistant came in and told me she was going to remove the two big tubes in my chest. After she got some gauze and tape, she told me to inhale deeply and then exhale slowly. During my exhale she was going to pull one of the tubes out and then repeat the process for the other one. I did what she said, but halfway through my first exhale, after pulling the eight-inch chest tube

66

halfway out, she realized she didn't have enough of the right gauze to bandage the wound after she took the tube out.

She then asked me to put pressure where the tube was halfway out of my chest while she ran to get whatever gear she forgot. I know I was probably only holding that pressure for thirty seconds at best, but it felt like an eternity until she returned.

When she came back, she pulled out the rest of the tube. I was not a happy patient after that escapade. Amanda was in the room and she was in shock over what she had just seen. In subsequent surgeries when I have had tubes removed, I always make sure the medical personnel have the needed bandages and relay this experience to them. I have a nice scar on my stomach reminding me of that unpleasant day.

I was in the hospital for thirteen days and when I came home I wasn't moving very quickly. After this procedure, I knew I had married someone who didn't take her wedding vows lightly. Amanda was willing to stay by me through sickness and in health. Never again did I doubt the love Amanda had for me. I knew after this that she will always love me despite my *Custom Scars*.

I was unable to do much of anything for more than four months and it took me close to a year to get enough strength back to even try to work full time. Many people encouraged me to apply for disability, but I wasn't going to let these scars hold me back. (I do have a fairly strong stubborn streak.) On the contrary, they motivated me to continue forward, as I knew there is a greater purpose for everything that happens. I knew God still had plans for my life.

CUSTOM SCARS & CUSTOM CARS

God has now added more custom pieces to my body so I can become more of whom my Maker (Creator) wants me to be. Just as my father is still cleaning up and assembling his *Custom Car* and it's becoming the car he desires it to be, my life's big picture is starting to take shape.

The 1948 Ford isn't all back together yet. It has a long way to go. It has many more chops and modifications to go through, just as I do. Since I am not completed yet, I wonder what other *Custom Scars* await me in the future?

seven

STILL LOVED WITH SCARS

Thankfully I was able to work part-time at a local Christian station, WAWN, while regaining my strength. It was nearly a year until I was able to work full time again after this surgery. Since I now had radio experience, I began sending my résumé to Christian radio stations primarily on the northeastern side of the United States. After three months I was hired in Syracuse, New York, at the Mars Hill Network.

When we moved, one of the first things we did was find the heart and pediatric doctors we needed. We also needed to find a midwife as we were expecting baby number two, Corban.

I was especially excited to hear that our second child was a boy. None of my Henry cousins had a son yet to continue on the family name, so I was thrilled to provide the first. Passing the Henry last name was important, but the origin of his first name held an even higher significance to me.

I was reading my Bible one day during my first year of college and came across Mark 7:11 where the word "Corban" is written and it means "a gift devoted to God." Right then, before I had even met Amanda, I knew what my firstborn son's name would be. All of our children's names have special meanings, but I knew Corban's before he was even born.

Life in Syracuse was definitely different than life in Papua New Guinea and northwestern Pennsylvania. Thankfully we were able to develop some good friendships with people at church and at work during our time there.

The three years we lived in Syracuse I never had any heart procedures or even concerns. Things seemed to be functioning really well heart-wise. For some reason, though, my one lung would partially collapse on a fairly regular basis. If you have ever experienced a collapsed lung, you know how painful it can be. With a collapsed lung, each breath in feels like a knife is being twisted under your ribs. The pulmonologist, lung doctor, couldn't figure out why it would deflate, and then within a day or two I would be fine. This happened three or four times while we lived in Syracuse, but other than that, my health held strong. Our third child, Dylan, was also born in 2005.

It was Spring 2006 when I was informed that a pastor from a church close to where I grew up was retiring. Roger Overmyer was his name, and I had spoken a few times about missions at his church. He had shared with me years earlier that if I ever felt called to be a pastor, he wanted me to talk with him so he could be an encouragement to me regarding God's leading. Since I had given everything over to God at that altar in Virginia, I was willing to go wherever God wanted and do whatever He wanted. I had actually driven from Syracuse twice to talk with Roger about the possibility of God calling me into the pastorate.

When I heard about his retirement, I sent my résumé to the church. My résumé consisted of a religion/communications degree, along with radio and missions experience. I had never been to seminary or pastored a church before. By this point in my life, I was the Program Director at the station and things in life were starting to settle down.

I was informed two months later that someone else had agreed to the terms of the church. All involved felt clear that the person they were hiring was the right person, and I was fine with that. It was enough for me to be obedient and send out my résumé. This rejection didn't make me lose hope either. Regardless of the decision, Amanda and I believed the Psalmist in Psalm 71:14, "But as for me, I will always have hope; I will praise you more and more."

Then, in October, I received a phone call that caught Amanda and me off guard. Ironically, it was the exact day of a house inspection for our first home we were looking to purchase in Syracuse. We had to either accept or reject the offer by the next day. God's timing is always perfect. Someone on the pastoral search committee at the church where I sent my résumé called and told me things had fallen through with the individual they thought they were hiring. As a result, the committee felt led to talk with me about the senior pastor position and wanted to know if I was still interested. I said that I was. So we stopped the process of buying a house in Syracuse and started to plan our move back to Northwest Pennsylvania.

I talked with Wayne Taylor, the station manager, about the direction we felt the Lord leading. He totally supported and encouraged me in this decision to return to Pennsylvania. He knew God opened the doors and he never wanted to hinder God's plan for my life.

When I interviewed at the church, I made it clear that they weren't getting the healthiest pastor. I did promise that with every ounce of strength and ability God gives me, I would do my best to lead this church in the direction the Lord wants it to go. Even after that health disclaimer, the pastoral search committee still felt strongly that I was to come.

On December 1, 2006 I became pastor of Victory Heights United Brethren in Christ Church in Franklin, Pennsylvania. We moved within twenty miles of my parents and most of my family. This was a new chapter in our lives. Since I was willing to do whatever God wanted me to do back at that camp in Danville, Virginia, the ministry change wasn't overwhelming.

The church welcomed this young twenty-eight-year-old kid with open arms. Roger Overmyer had laid a wonderful foundation during his twenty-two years of ministry at the church. He also made an incredible and noticeable impact within the community. It was difficult when Roger retired and then here comes a young man with no pastoral experience. God knew what He was doing and I am thankful for His leading us back home to my roots. I am also thankful for the patience of many within the church.

It wasn't long until we had our fourth child, Andrew, in 2008 and were looking into buying our first house. We were living in the church parsonage, but felt it best to live somewhere other than right beside the church. The size of the house and the growth of the family added to this decision.

During that same time, we found out I had another AAA, this time on the lower half of my aorta. With another imminent surgery on the horizon, we closed on a house a couple of miles from the church in order to be settled in before the next procedure. It was a busy time, but having a place to call our own was a blessing.

So at this point, we were living in our new home and making game plans for my next abdominal aortic aneurysm surgery. The surgeon told us he would replace my descending aorta from the point where the last surgery left off and go the whole way down to where the aorta splits off into the two main arteries in my legs. It was in the spring of 2009, when I was thirty-one, the surgeons did another AAA, entering my chest the same way the last surgeon did in the previous surgery, through my left side.

I had a good idea what the surgeon was going to do and how I was going to feel after the procedure, but surprisingly enough, this time I didn't hurt nearly as bad! The surgeon, Dr. Chess, did add an additional twelve inches of new scar on my left side, but the rest of the incision was where my existing scar was. It was nice to not have too many "new" marks.

I thought it was incredible that I could have pretty much the same surgery yet with a very different recovery process. I had prepared for a long and painful recovery but was pleasantly surprised when I experienced significantly less pain the second time around. Praise the Lord.

My hospital stay wasn't as long but, again, Amanda stayed with me the entire time. Our family helped so much in caring for our children in order for Amanda to stay with me in the hospital. The grandparents busied themselves keeping track of our four children. Amanda's love during my recovery sped up my healing time. She is someone special, and I cannot truly express my gratitude to God for giving her to me.

The nurses in the hospital take care of so many people that they were not always able to help right when I needed them. Amanda was there to help me with my meals, to the restroom, and with anything else I needed. When I was blessed with her as my wife, I didn't have a clue what she would do for me without hesitation.

A good friend from the church, John, came to stay with me one night so Amanda could get a good night's sleep at a nearby hotel. He even paid for her room! I didn't get a good rest that night because John snored, but his act of kindness was pivotal for Amanda to get some needed sleep. John's friendship, just like Amy's when I was a teenager, reassured me that people loved me for who I am. I am loved with my *Custom Scars*.

(As you know, sometimes family or friends cannot be with you or your loved one after surgery. This is another issue I stress to medical students: to be there for your patients because they might not have anyone else. Sometimes the medical staff is the only glimmer of hope a patient has.)

I made the trip back home from the hospital in ten days, but it was weeks before I could pick up any of my children. We now had four children who had a hard time not jumping on and playing with Dad. It was difficult when my children just wanted Dad to play on the floor with them, but even getting on the floor was painful . . . let alone playing! Amanda was very patient with the children and taught them how to act around me until I got better.

The church was incredibly supportive during my time off. They brought us meals and supported us in every possible way. Many in the church helped with the children, my duties and responsibilities at the church, and just about anything else you can imagine!

With my previous AAA, the incision had been glued closed and I didn't have any stitches or staples. With my second AAA, the surgeon used more than sixty staples to close my incision. I was very surprised when I saw the number of staples along my side. Our children were fascinated with them as well. They called it "Daddy's zipper." When I first came home and started back to church, the younger kids would ask people if they wanted to see Daddy's zipper! I told them that probably wasn't the best idea because no one needs to see Daddy's zipper. I also told them they shouldn't call my staples Daddy's zipper in public. The looks of confusion directed at me when my children talked about Daddy's zipper were interesting. It's funny how our children can classify and perceive things. I was relieved to have those staples removed, making Daddy's zipper disappear. The holes where the staples went in, however, created more than a hundred little scars.

That year, 2009, was a difficult year apart from buying a house and having another major surgery. My father-in-law, Tim, had been battling stage four pancreatic cancer for over three long years during a time when he still had four daughters in school. Tim and Cindy, my mother-in-law, routinely traveled to Baltimore, Maryland from western Ohio, so that Tim could try various treatments to slow down the progress of the cancer.

Throughout those years, Tim fought hard to stay with his family. He tried experimental treatments as he was given only months to live. I not only had a wonderful wife during my surgeries, but I also had wonderful in-laws and Tim was always encouraging me before and after those procedures. He would do anything to help his favorite son-in-law (as I was his only son-in-law), his daughter, and his only grandchildren.

After the second AAA, Tim and Cindy and the family came to our house a number of times that summer. We had a pool and I remember swimming and Tim and my dad sitting on top of the hill above the pool just watching the kids and grandkids swimming. When my dad and my father-in-law got together they never had a problem talking. I knew when our families got together a couple of times a year that Tim and my dad wouldn't ever run out of topics to discuss! Whether it was cars, machines, or faith, the conversations flowed easily.

The last time Tim and Cindy and all my wife's sisters came to our house was on May 25, 2009. That was also the day of the last family picture taken of all the children, grandchildren, and of course Tim's favorite son-in-law.

As fall approached, Tim's health was steadily declining. Treatment options had been exhausted, and we were now faced with the inevitable fact that the time our family had on this earth with my favorite father-in-law was dwindling down.

The first weekend in October 2009, we packed up our children and went to visit Grandma and Grandpa Campitelli. They lived near Canton, Ohio, and it was only an hour and forty-five-minute trip to get to their house. That Friday night Tim ate supper with the family but then started not feeling well throughout the evening. At this time we had a feeling this was the beginning of the final days for Tim. We then drove the children back over to my parents and a couple from the church in Pennsylvania to look after them so we could stay in Ohio with my in-laws.

There I was, scarred from the bullying of my childhood, scarred from the loss of my mother so many years ago from cancer, scarred from the multiple surgeries over the last decade. Now I was going to have to deal with the scars of losing my father-in-law.

I do have one regret during those last days of Tim's life. He always wanted to take me to the Pro Football Hall of Fame in Canton, Ohio. It was only a few miles away from where he and Cindy lived. He wanted to go there with his only son, as he and Cindy had six daughters.

I always told Tim, "We can go later." I now know I was in denial (just as I was with my mother) that he wasn't going to die. I figured if I pushed back the date for us to go, he would just keep living until he was well enough for us to make the trip. That was a mistake. Seize the days you have with the ones you love. Treat each day as if it may be your last because you cannot go back in time and our actions have consequences.

Scars in our lives do affect us. Sometimes the scars distort our thinking, and our actions reflect that distortion. Sadly, and regretfully, I never took the opportunity to go to the Hall of Fame with Tim. I cannot change that fact, but I have learned from that mistake. You never know how much time you have with someone. You must use the time you do have with the people you love constructively.

Those final days with Tim were difficult. There I was with my wife and her family as this pivotal man in their lives, Grandpa and Dad, was slowly slipping from this life into eternity. We had no doubt Tim would spend eternity in Heaven when he passed because he had a real, personal relationship with Jesus. That is the hope a Christian has. Tim quickly declined to a point where he wasn't able to eat or drink. His communications and functions were deteriorating rapidly. I would sit beside him as he lay on the hospital bed in the dining room area. He responded well to me as I swabbed his mouth with a small sponge so he could get a little bit of water on his tongue. His lips were so dry and his mouth so parched as he quickly slipped into an unresponsive state. I will never forget those precious final days of sitting beside a man who didn't think or believe anything less of me because of my scars, giving him drops of water in his mouth. We are to give love and comfort to the end to whoever needs it.

Those few days were tough as Tim was fading into eternity. All of his children were there, as well as Tim's parents and one brother and sister-in-law. We spent a lot of time talking and preparing as best we could for what was to come. We cherished those final moments that we were able to share with Tim.

Then on Thursday, October 8, 2009, just after midnight, Tim met my mom for the first time as he left this world to spend eternity with Jesus in Heaven. He was only fifty years old. Most of his children were still in school and college. Four grandchildren were left without Grandpa Campitelli, but as I said when I faced the death of my mother, death is an inevitable reality in our lives. It is not a respecter of age.

When a loved one dies, emptiness fills your life. You are often at a loss as to how to deal with this void. It's an emptiness I hadn't felt in sixteen years, an emptiness I hadn't felt since the day my mother died. Even though I knew both my father-in-law and my mother were in Heaven, it still didn't make their departures easy.

Now another emotional scar had taken place, though it left a deeper scar on my wife than it did me because this was her father.

We shared the same scar together but in differing degrees. I wanted to be there for my wife and her family during this time of loss, but it was so hard because I was having a difficult time with my own feelings and emotions. Tim's strength through this trial affected all of us, yet we could find strength in the hope of his eternal destination.

This time was also difficult for our children because Grandpa was gone. They cried at the funeral, and Amanda and I talked with each of them about their feelings and what had happened. I knew from my experience that kids need honesty. Keeping the realities of life and death away from them hinders their healing. Even now the older children talk about Grandpa Campitelli, but, as time passes, those memories will fade, just as the memories of my mother have faded. Tim loved me and was proud that someone with these *Custom Scars* married his daughter.

CUSTOM SCARS & CUSTOM CARS

That year was quite difficult with a major surgery and the death of my father-in-law. It seemed like life was proceeding fine and then I got hit with a curveball. A surgery can be processed much easier and quicker than death.

It was almost as if the strength (or work) we had put into building something had been taken away, as if the garage had burned down when Dad was halfway finished building his 1948 Ford. I have been comparing my dad's *Custom Car* to my *Custom Scars* and the building being done, but when Tim died, honestly, seeing the finished product in my life and the lives of the family was like my emotional garage burnt down. The question we often ask is just one word: "Why?"

Many times we never find an answer to that question. Even so, we must hold firmly to the fact that God will help us through times like these. He is the one who can use these difficult situations we all face that produce hope through our *Custom Scars*.

eight

SCARRED CHILDREN

The loss of Grandpa Campitelli was incredibly difficult for our family. I had to explain to our children, now one, three, five, and seven years old, that their Grandpa was gone, he had died, and that they wouldn't be able to go visit with him again. I was struggling to be strong for them as I was experiencing the same hurt and loss. The emotions I hadn't felt in more than a decade came barreling back in an almost unbearable way. How was I supposed to comfort such young children? How could I help bring hope to a hopeless situation? How was I supposed to help them with the scars of death when I was facing that same battle? How could I be the husband I needed to be for Amanda?

God's love and comfort helped, or maybe I should say carried, us through this difficult time. We didn't hide the realities of death from our children, and they wept bitterly when they saw Grandpa Campitelli's body at his funeral service. We also didn't hide the reality that he is no longer in pain. We reassured them, as did all that was said and done during his funeral service, that Grandpa Campitelli is in Heaven because of his commitment to Jesus. This is such an incredible hope that we could share with our children in this time of loss. A hope that if they make the same commitment to Jesus Christ, they will see their Grandpa Campitelli again and spend eternity in Heaven.

Tim's life verses were 2 Timothy 4:1-8:

In the presence of God and of Christ Jesus, who will judge the living and the dead, and in view of his appearing and his kingdom, I give you this charge: 2 Preach the Word; be prepared in season and out of season; correct, rebuke and encourage—with great patience and careful instruction. 3 For the time will come when men will not put up with sound doctrine. Instead, to suit their own desires, they will gather around them a great number of teachers to say what their itching ears want to hear. 4 They will turn their ears away from the truth and turn aside to myths. 5 But you, keep your head in all situations, endure hardship, do the work of an evangelist, discharge all the duties of your ministry.

6 For I am already being poured out like a drink offering, and the time has come for my departure. 7 I have fought the good fight, I have finished the race, I have kept the faith. 8 Now there is in store for me the crown of righteousness, which the Lord, the righteous Judge, will award to me on that day—and not only to me, but also to all who have longed for his appearing.

Scars don't respect age, and my young children are now accumulating their own scars. They've had to live through the effects that Marfan syndrome had on my life, adjusting what we can and can't do due to some of my limitations, and now they had to process the scars of losing their grandpa. As a father and husband, it is imperative that I remain strong for my family so they have someone to lean on for strength, even when I am struggling on the inside. It is not always easy.

Life doesn't stop even when we get scarred. At this time we had four children, and since Marfan syndrome is a genetic condition, we needed to find out if its scars had been passed down to any of them. Medical technology had advanced since my diagnosis, so all doctors needed to do was take a sample of my blood and compare it to samples of my children's blood and an accurate Marfan diagnosis could be given regarding our children.

Exploring our options for this type of testing, we found a wonderful geneticist, Dr. Madan, at Children's Hospital of Pittsburgh. She welcomed us as new patients and encouraged us to have this type of testing performed on our children. She has loved our family from the first time we met her and is a wonderful friend and supporter. Dr. Madan has shown our family genuine concern as we live with Marfan syndrome.

After the scheduling had been made for the five of us (me and my four children) to have our blood drawn, the wait started. Amanda and I were fairly certain our middle son, Dylan, would be positively diagnosed because he has many of the physical characteristics of a Marfan patient. The other children we weren't as sure about, so we just had to wait for the official results. Our two oldest children, Michaela and Corban, tested negative for Marfan syndrome. Neither of them exhibited any outward symptoms of the condition, so we weren't surprised by this result. As we had assumed, Dylan was positively diagnosed with Marfan syndrome, and somewhat surprisingly, his younger brother, Andrew, was also. In 2010 we had our fifth and final child, Jana, and she tested negative like her two oldest siblings.

We now have the privilege and opportunity to raise two boys with Marfan syndrome. Amanda knew before we were married that our children had a 50% chance of having this condition. I made sure she was forewarned. Amanda had been by my side through two major surgeries, but thankfully that didn't deter her from being the mother of my children. We both knew there was a real possibility that some or all of our children could be diagnosed with Marfan syndrome. If they were anything like me, they would probably need to have some major medical procedures done in order for them to live fuller lives. Regardless of those concerns, we now have five beautiful children who are loved with their *Custom Scars*. Since I have lived life with Marfan syndrome, I can also be a pivotal support and example for my children on how to thrive with a positive Marfan diagnosis. Dylan and Andrew should have an advantage that wasn't available for me growing up.

Amanda and I believe very strongly that all the children God has allowed us to rear were created for a purpose. God created them exactly how He intended them to be. It didn't matter to Amanda if our children were like their father, as she loved me regardless of Marfan syndrome. Her love and strength for our family through all the mountains and the valleys is pivotal to our family's bond.

It has been a number of years since we were definitively told the news that Dylan and Andrew have Marfan syndrome. Dylan clearly has most of the outward signs. His chest is incredibly concave. He is tall and thin, just like I was when I was his age. When you put my old school pictures beside his pictures, we could pass for twins. Dylan has almost the textbook look for someone with Marfan syndrome. Although Andrew is a very tall boy, he doesn't as clearly exhibit the distinguishing skeletal characteristics of Marfan's like his older brother does.

Marfan syndrome isn't just about external differences. The boys' aortas are top priority, especially considering how much trouble I have had with mine. We make sure we schedule their yearly appointments with their geneticist, their pediatric ophthalmologist, and their pediatric cardiologist. As someone who has been diagnosed and treated with a manageable condition, I understand the importance of regular checkups. It is vital that the boys are regularly checked for outward and inward changes related to Marfan syndrome.

The boys have an EKG and an echocardiogram done each year to see if any changes in their aortic valves or their aortas have occurred. When Andrew was three years old it was deemed best to start him on a beta-blocker, since his aortic root appeared slightly enlarged. He was fairly young to be showing these signs, but he was a trooper and started taking a small pill each morning at breakfast to help reduce the strain on his aorta. A year after Andrew started his beta-blocker, Dylan started on the same pill each morning as a precaution to preserve his aorta too.

Thinking back on my childhood days, I know what it was like to not be able to participate in some of the activities that my friends could. I also knew what it was like to be teased for not looking like the rest of my peers. I do my best to help my boys not have to experience those same feelings. I know I can't protect them from everything, and they will experience disappointments in their lives due to having Marfan syndrome, but what they do with their disappointments is controllable; and I have a wonderful opportunity to guide them down the paths for success.

Amanda and I have done our best to find things they enjoy doing within their activity limitations. It can be difficult, but we try to be creative and direct them toward those means. Bike riding is a good activity, as is fishing. Swimming is encouraged for Marfan's patients, as it doesn't put strain on the joints. Many of the places where we have lived had access to a swimming pool, which all of our children gravitated towards.

It is also a blessing to have a large family because the kids play and do things with each other. The entire family understands the limits that Marfan syndrome can have, and we work hard to include everyone in family activities. When love and acceptance of who God has made us to be is demonstrated and encouraged in home life, the children don't need much more to know they are special.

Amanda and I make sure Dylan and Andrew know they have physical limitations. We also make them keenly aware of the signs they need to know to slow down a little. Since they will be limited in their professions, we do our best to explore available futures. We also encourage them to use the abilities they do have and are allowed to use for their betterment, the betterment of others, and for God's glory.

> **I want my boys to look at me and know that Marfan syndrome isn't going to define me, that despite some limitations, I am defined by who I am as a Christian.**

When the boys were really young, we correlated that Daddy has Marfan's to help them understand themselves. This can be a little scary for the boys since I have had a number of surgeries. Thankfully though, I can direct them to the fact that they can still achieve a great deal in life even though they have a genetic condition. There is hope, especially in our faith. I want my boys to look at me and know that Marfan syndrome isn't going to define me, that despite some limitations, I am defined by who I am as a Christian.

My heart goes out to all the children whose parents don't love them because of an uncontrollable condition they may have. But I give a great big applause to parents who love their children with all their hearts even though they may have a severe physical limitation. You inspire me and inspire many others. Keep on loving no matter what.

Our oldest son, Corban, has played flag football and basketball for a number of years. He really enjoys playing sports and is improving each year. Some of the other parents at the games ask Andrew and Dylan if they are excited to be able to play like their big brother. I always anticipate (and dread) hearing how they will respond to this question. It's the real test to see whether we are doing something right in parenting children with a unique health concern.

I love what Dylan typically says in one form or another. He will say something like, "No, I can't play sports. I'm like my dad. We have Marfan syndrome, so we can't do some of those things," in a matter-of-fact kind of way. I do find it funny because he says it as if the person asking the question actually knows something about Marfan syndrome.

Just because someone may be physically limited in one way or another, it doesn't mean that person has no purpose or use.

I just roll my eyes and chuckle. The opportunity then arises to share with the parent that we have a heart issue that doesn't allow us to play contact sports. Just because someone may be physically limited in one way or another, it doesn't mean that person has no purpose or use.

Dylan looks at me, his father, as an example for him. The more he is like his daddy, the better! Would the two younger boys like to be able to do what their older brother does? By all means they would, but since they have limits, the same limits I had, we find plenty of other activities to do.

How you teach, encourage, and love your children who are not "normal" makes an immeasurable impact on the future of your kids. Remember, we are all normal because we are just as God intended us to be, so there is actually no such thing as "normal." My heart and mind continue to go back to Psalm 139:14: "I praise you because I am fearfully and wonderfully made; your works are wonderful, I know that full well." I am exactly how God wants me to be and I must be willing to accept myself because God already has. How are you living and loving life with the blessings (and sometimes challenges) that come with a unique physical condition?

I hope you have noticed by now that I haven't referred to Marfan syndrome as a disability. Maybe I'm wrong for not calling it that. I know that many others who experience daily differences in life from "normal" people feel the same way about using that word. Do our two sons and I have some limits others may not? Yes! That doesn't mean any of us are less of a person because of those limits.

My heart is saddened by the state of American society when it comes to the value of human life. At this point, I have had three life-saving surgeries. My family has gone through significant emotional pain while I am acquiring my scars that have given me life. All life—the unborn, the uniquely created, and the "normal"—are all special

88

and worth protecting and saving. From the time of conception, we are wonderfully made the way God has chosen us to be. How are you loving and caring for those living around you?

Neither of the boys with Marfan syndrome have had any surgeries in their young lives. I have talked to them some about my surgeries and told them they will probably have one or more in the future. Since I have a pretty good idea what they should and shouldn't do, I will hopefully be able to postpone surgical procedures for them until they are at least in high school. I encourage them that medical advances are so incredible that maybe by the time they need to have any of the procedures I have had done, they could be substantially less invasive.

Dylan and Andrew may have the *Custom Scars* of Marfan syndrome, but with all my strength and ability, I want to guide them to know that Marfan's will not dictate who they will become. Marfan syndrome will not defeat them. If they look for their strength in God, they will be able to accomplish incredible things regardless of this condition their father passed onto them.

CUSTOM SCARS & CUSTOM CARS

As I stated previously, my dad rebuilt a couple of other vehicles—a 1957 Chevy Nomad and a 1955 Chevy step-side pickup—before he started customizing his 1948 Ford. My father also worked on cars when he was a teenager and, actually, all his life. He has a great deal of firsthand experience as a mechanic. That experience and wisdom typically helps him with his projects.

Some of the modifications my Dad wanted to do on his 1948 Ford were beyond his abilities. He sought out people who could do major custom bodywork. Dad couldn't paint the car or reupholster its interior, for example, so he found people to help him where his weaknesses were. He could do a lot of the work, but even in building his *Custom Car*, he needed other people to help him finish the project.

Since I have Marfan syndrome, I have experienced living life the way my sons will have to live theirs. This gives me that "hands-on" experience, which will hopefully give me the advantage my parents did not have when I was growing up. I cannot build up my children alone on their journey with their *Custom Scars*. We utilize medical specialists that keep current on advancements and treatments of Marfan syndrome. This gives Amanda and I the resources we need to decide on what the best treatments need to be. The love of grandparents, family, neighbors, teachers, and friends that is shown to them, regardless of their *Custom Scars*, also builds up their self-esteem and confidence that they can succeed.

My dad could have never finished his *Custom Car* alone. He did most of the work, but he needed some support. Amanda and I will do most of the work regarding the two boys who have Marfan's, but it is a blessing to have others walking with us to help our children with their *Custom Scars*.

nine

THE FINAL SCAR?

The scars I'd experienced up to this point were ones I had some time to prepare and plan for. I might not have had months or years, but I was at least able to prepare for the scars that were coming. That preparation wasn't going to happen when the winter of 2010 came blowing into our little town. But before we get to that life-altering event, I need to lay a little foundation about our life earlier that year.

In June our second daughter, and final child, was born. We now have two girls and three boys. Since the two youngest boys have Marfan syndrome, we decided Jana would be our last biological child. We wanted to make sure we could properly care for all five of our children. The day after Jana was born I saw my cardiologist, Dr. Maher, for my yearly checkup. I had an EKG, an echocardiogram, and met with the doctor by myself because Amanda had just given birth to Jana and was still in the hospital. Dr. Maher proceeded to tell me the valve that was replaced when I was eighteen (back in 1997) showed significant signs of stiffening up and its movement wasn't as fluid as it needed to be. Something would probably need to be done shortly to remedy the problem, but in the meantime, we would keep a close eye on it. If I experienced any odd pains or discomfort, I needed to get it checked out immediately.

When I got back to the hospital, I told Amanda the tests showed nothing out of the ordinary. I didn't say that to intentionally lie to her; I had simply forgotten what the doctor said about my valve. I heard Dr. Maher say things might eventually need fixing but didn't take it to heart that my valve could actually cease to function anytime in the immediate future. Truth be told, my listening and communication skills needed further development.

Summer turned to fall and fall turned to winter in northwestern Pennsylvania. We had a mild Thanksgiving, but after that, the snow came in pretty quick. I don't remember many dates in my life, but I will never forget that Sunday morning, December 5, 2010. I was thirty-two years old. That night a couple of inches of light snow had accumulated and I wanted to push it off the driveway before we headed to church. I took the dog out of his pen in the basement and to his large outdoor pen behind the house. Ironically, we had a special group that Sunday so I didn't have to preach. I was just going to enjoy listening to the Sunday morning service with my family.

Not long after I started removing the snow from the driveway, I began to feel fatigued. Since I wasn't preaching that morning, I figured I could expend a little more energy before church to clear off the driveway. After half of the drive was clear, my chest got really tight and started to hurt. The breath was taken right out of me. Winded and perplexed, I leaned on the shovel in the driveway. While I was leaning against the shovel, the sky burst open and it started snowing really hard. Big beautiful snowflakes were negating the work I had just accomplished, but it was beautiful! I stood there for a couple of minutes trying to catch my breath, but the short rest didn't relieve any of the symptoms or discomfort I was experiencing. Since the snow was really starting to come down and I wasn't feeling well at all, I made my way back inside the house. Our vehicle was an all-wheel drive, which would still make it possible for us to get to church even though I didn't get all the snow removed.

I grabbed an armful of wood to take to the woodburner in the basement. I came in the basement door, removed my boots, and took the wood to the woodburner. I sat in front of the fire and stoked it a little to get warmed up. With the shortness of breath and increased discomfort, I ended up lying on the basement floor for a few minutes. Amanda and the kids were upstairs unaware that anything was happening. Since no relief had occurred for ten minutes, I knew something unusual was going on. I sluggishly made my way upstairs and informed Amanda about the chain of events that had just occurred and how I was feeling.

As you know, Amanda has been by my side through a number of physical challenges and surgeries. I told her that these feelings and pain just weren't right and they weren't like anything I had ever experienced before. She was now becoming very concerned. I had never felt something like this, it wasn't going away, and I was having a hard time even thinking straight. It was also gradually getting harder to catch my breath, and even harder to breathe. She asked me not once, not twice, but three times if she should call an ambulance. I knew something was seriously wrong, so after the third time I told her to make the call.

After the call, Amanda contacted my parents and asked them to come take care of the children in order for her to be at the hospital with me. By this time it was just after 8 a.m. and the snow was coming down in blizzard fashion. It seemed like the ambulance took forever to get to our house. I kept asking Amanda if it had arrived yet, as I was feeling progressively worse. Everything was getting tighter in my chest, and the ability to breathe was becoming strenuous. Something was seriously wrong and my entire family was witnessing it. Were my children, ages eight, six, five, two, and our five-month-old baby, about to watch their father die in front of their eyes? The rapid regression of my breathing and the ever-increasing tightness in my chest seemed to indicate this might be the end of life's journey for me.

I vividly remember my oldest daughter, Michaela, standing in the hallway, looking at me with intense concern and then breaking down in tears as she ran to her room. The older kids were crying because they didn't know if Daddy was dying. Seeing that type of pain in my children is one of my most difficult memories pertaining to this event. I cannot imagine the scars it left on them. The hopelessness in their eyes was crushing. Without some immediate medical intervention, I began thinking that I may be dying. An ambulance was slowly making its way to our home on this blustery day but the weather delayed its arrival.

At last the ambulance pulled into the bottom of the lane, but by this time the snow had made the lane up to our house practically impassable. After a handful of attempts, the ambulance made it up the lane to the bottom of our driveway but couldn't make it up to our home. The emergency personnel trekked up our drive, through the basement, and made their way upstairs where I was waiting. We gave them a brief rundown of what had happened, and they did their initial vitals evaluation.

Because of the weather conditions, they asked if I thought I could walk to the ambulance. I said I thought I could. With the help of the EMTs, I walked down the basement stairs, out the basement door, and down our short driveway to the waiting ambulance. The EMTs quickly loaded me into the ambulance where I answered their questions in more detail about what had just happened. With each minute and breath I took, things were becoming more confusing and breathing more labored.

Our lane was practically buried with snow. The descent down was treacherous. The ambulance slid all over the road. Winter upkeep was always a concern, but with this sudden snowstorm, the journey down was as difficult as coming up. Due to the heavy snowfall, it took the ambulance fifteen minutes to drive the five miles to the hospital.

While I was en route, Amanda contacted someone from the church to let them know something serious had happened to me and we would not be there for the special service. Then she waited for my parents to arrive at the house to take care of the children so she could get to the emergency room.

The emergency room nurse on duty was Mrs. Kellogg. She was the mother of a high school friend of mine. Mrs. Kellogg is a wonderful Christian woman and I knew she would make sure I would receive the best care. I was so happy to have someone with me whom I knew since Amanda was still waiting for my parents to arrive at our home. The ER staff was busily trying to figure out what was going on inside me and which diagnostic or treatment options they needed in order to stabilize me.

They knew quickly that whatever was going on was beyond their expertise and that they needed to send me to a facility equipped to handle my complicated medical background. They wanted to life flight me to Pittsburgh, but the snowy weather was too severe that all the helicopters were grounded. I made sure they knew all my doctors were at Allegheny General Hospital in Pittsburgh and to contact them immediately.

The symptoms appeared to be that of a heart attack, but in all my years of checkups, I had never had a single issue with my heart. Marfan syndrome had affected my aorta, but not my actual heart muscle. In light of the symptoms, however, the ER staff treated my condition like a heart attack.

I had been at the hospital an hour before Amanda was able to get there, though my dad had already arrived. By this point the ER staff had hooked me up to an IV to give me drugs for the pain. My blood work indicated I was having a heart attack. But was I? That conclusion just didn't make sense to Amanda or me.

The ER doctor moved me to a trauma room to keep a closer watch on my condition, as my breathing was deteriorating rapidly. By this time they had contacted my doctors at Allegheny General Hospital (AGH) in Pittsburgh to help with my diagnosis and possible treatment. The doctor at our local hospital wanted to give me a clot buster, but my doctors in Pittsburgh stated that wasn't a good idea with Marfan's because if it wasn't a heart attack, the clot buster might make the situation worse. After some disagreements, the local ER doctor deferred those decisions to my specialists in Pittsburgh.

Not long after that discussion, I started coughing up blood—which isn't a heart attack symptom—and my oxygen levels dropped drastically. At this point, the ER doctors knew I needed to get to Pittsburgh quickly, but in the meantime, they asked my wife and father to leave the room while they stabilized me. Since coughing up blood indicated my lungs were filling up, they decided to insert a breathing tube.

Since the helicopter was grounded, the ER staff was trying to stabilize me enough so that I could take an ambulance to Pittsburgh. Each minute of not knowing what was happening to me seemed like an eternity for my family. Would one of these minutes be my final one on this earth? Was I actually dying?

The medical team that rode in the ambulance with me were the medical professionals who would normally ride in the helicopter. They weren't just the regular EMTs (which I am so grateful for) but highly trained individuals, prepared for the unknowns of what may happen when someone is experiencing extreme trauma.

It wasn't even lunchtime as I was being loaded into the ambulance. In a matter of four hours I went from doing the morning chores to being completely helpless. I was heavily sedated and on a breathing tube by the time we left for Pittsburgh, with my lungs still filling up with blood. Definitely not what I pictured my day would be like when I picked that snow shovel up a few hours prior. Amanda, our five-month-old daughter, Jana, and my father left for Pittsburgh, too.

During this time, Amanda had contacted her mom to let her know what was going on and told her to pray. Cindy told the Lord that even though she knew Tim, my father-in-law, was in heaven with Him, she could not lose me, too. Maybe that was a selfish prayer, but God understands our hearts, and I am so glad I have a mother-in-law who will petition God for the life of her son-in-law. Romans 12:12 states, "Be joyful in hope, patient in affliction, faithful in prayer." Our family clung to these words from Scripture during this time more than they ever had before.

The trip was treacherous for both the ambulance and my family. God's grace protected us all and we made it to Pittsburgh by early afternoon. My diagnosis was still unknown and the emergency room doctors at Allegheny General Hospital tried to narrow down what was happening.

By the time Amanda made it to AGH, I was in the Coronary Care Unit where the staff was trying to figure out if I actually did have a heart attack or if it was something else related to Marfan syndrome. The surgeon asked Amanda a multitude of questions about how I had been feeling. My levels had stabilized significantly on the trip down to AGH; now we just needed a correct diagnosis and treatment to be able to move forward. The medical team felt that since I was stable, all the pieces needed to be put together correctly before they would act on any major treatment.

After all the questions had been answered the best we knew how, the doctor felt it best to wait until Monday to do a transesophageal echocardiogram (TEE) to see what damage may have occurred to my heart. Although the staff still believed it could be a heart attack, the cardiologist was starting to seriously question that diagnosis.

By Sunday evening, I had stabilized and was starting to become somewhat coherent. I was on a breathing machine and very concerned that I was still at the local hospital and not in Pittsburgh. It took a while for my mind to realize I was at AGH and that the team of doctors knew my history and were working to figure out what had happened. My father, wife, and daughter went home that night to get some rest and for Amanda to pack some clothes for what we assumed was going to be an extended hospital stay.

On Monday, the TEE indeed showed I did NOT have a heart attack. Rather, the aortic valve replaced in 1997 had torn. Apparently, the valve (the one I forgot to mention anything to Amanda about after my appointment with Dr. Maher) decided its lifespan was up! One of the three leaflets had torn. It didn't tear off completely, but was held on by only a small piece. When one of the three leaflets in your aortic valve tear, it causes substantial strain on one's body. My blood was continually washing back into my lungs since the damaged valve wasn't functioning correctly. My heart muscles were fine, but the homograph valve that was grafted in needed to come out soon, and a St. Jude's artificial valve needed to be grafted in its place.

Dr. Magovern, the same surgeon who performed my first valve replacement in 1997, told Amanda he wasn't going to perform the aortic valve replacement surgery until Thursday. Even though my wife couldn't believe he was going to wait four days, my body needed to recover some from the trauma it had experienced from the tear. He also wanted to make sure he had the best team of professionals there to ensure the valve replacement went smoothly. He reassured my wife that if for some reason I took a turn for the worse, he would not hesitate to perform the surgery sooner. He believed I was stable enough, however, to wait until all the right people were in place. Amanda understood what needed to be done and agreed with the doctor's directives. She respected his professional opinion completely.

I have very little memory of those four days. While waiting for the surgery, I was on a breathing machine to limit the amount of work my body had to do to survive because blood was still washing back into my lungs from the torn aortic valve. The only time it wasn't irritating was when I pulled out the tube and asked for pizza and pop. The nursing staff wasn't happy with that and quickly replaced the tube. I've been told I was coherent during these days and that I communicated with visitors and the doctor by writing things on a piece of paper on a clipboard. My vague memories make the experience seem like it was a dream within a dream.

The medical staff had justifiable concerns about pneumonia and fever the days before the surgery, and with that in mind, they worked diligently to make sure I was staying strong. The biggest concern was the continued blood in my lungs. I would write on my paper "suffocating," which meant I felt like I was drowning in my own blood. The nurse would then put a suction tube down my breathing tube and suck the blood out of my lungs. I was supposed to be fully sedated during these times, but they gave me the maximum amount of sedation they felt they could safely give me, and yet I was still awake. One of the nurses told my wife the amount of sedatives the staff gave me could have literally taken down a rhino. I have a high tolerance for sedatives and pain. I don't enjoy pain, but with these types of situations that have happened in my life, I am thankful I can tolerate it.

I remember the feeling of drowning and the pain my body experienced as the nurses would remove the fluid from my lungs. That is a memory I wish I could eradicate. Amanda had a hard time being there because every time they removed the fluid from my lungs, my entire body shook due to the severe pain. I can't fathom what she went through emotionally by being by my side. Never once did she walk away, and every time I needed her she was there. Since that experience, whenever I hear about drowning, I flash back to when I was drowning in my own blood and cringe at the memory.

Those days of waiting caused great stress and concern for my family, as they waited and watched me in such critical shape. The faith of my wife was incredible. Even though it wasn't easy she came to a point where she left it all in God's hands. Hebrews 10:23 says, "Let us hold unswervingly to the hope we profess, for he who promised is faithful." Those promises were what Amanda held onto during these days.

Because of the way I looked, connected to all the machines, Amanda and I decided to not let the children see me until after the surgery. This was a scar-producing time in their lives, as they had to trust that Daddy would be fine even though they couldn't visit me. Many great nurses and doctors helped me through this and served as an incredible support system for my wife and family.

The day finally came for them to graft in my new valve. When Amanda spoke with a medical resident who was in the operating room during my valve replacement surgery, he told her he had never seen so many senior-level cardiologists, surgeons, and anesthesiologists working on one patient. It was the A+++ team of Allegheny General Hospital for heart surgery.

The preparation was thorough, and the surgery went quickly, as we had been waiting four days for that top-level medical staff to perform it. Dr. Thomas Maher, my cardiologist's husband, and a top cardiothoracic surgeon at Allegheny General Hospital, sat with

Amanda and my family shortly after the surgery. He told them my aortic valve had indeed torn. He was amazed it was functioning at all because it had the consistency and texture of a Styrofoam cup. Later Dr. Magovern reassured my wife and family that all went better than expected. I even had less scar tissue from my previous surgeries than the staff had anticipated, which made the surgery progress faster and easier. (If you want to use the word "miracle" here, I think it would fit.)

Everyone on the medical team was quite pleased with the outcome and the start of my post-op recovery. Amanda had asked my surgeon, as I did later, what my chances were of surviving this tear. His answer was always, "Once you were at Allegheny General Hospital and stable, we had no doubts that you would make a full recovery." I owe my life to Dr. Magovern and the incredible medical teams I have had at Allegheny General Hospital. Without their life-saving skills, who knows whether I would still be alive.

The medical staff kept me fully sedated the Thursday of my surgery and didn't actually close my incision until Friday. I remember waking up Saturday and being really confused. I actually thought I was dead and in hell, though I have no idea why.

I remember all sorts of Christmas decorations in the ICU recovery room. There were decorations on the desks, on the counters, and hanging from the ceilings. In my confusion, I thought one of the nurses named "Nick" was Santa Claus. I asked him to help me get out of there because I was in hell and Satan (another nurse) was coming back! I am not going to talk anymore about Nurse Lucifer, but she wasn't very nice to me or my family when they visited.

"Nick" didn't set me free, but he was very kind to me in my confusion. Over the next thirty-six hours, my family came in during visiting hours and helped me understand what had happened. I was still so confused. I didn't know where I was or what had happened to me. Once the staff moved me from ICU (or "hell," as I thought) and into my own room, it was like Heaven, especially because the Steelers' game was on when I arrived! Amanda also greatly helped me begin to put the pieces of the last week together.

Turns out the ICU wasn't hell, and many wonderful people took care of me while I was there, at least that's what my wife told me. The real recovery had begun now that I was in my own room and becoming more aware of what had happened over the last week.

Exactly one week had elapsed from the time my valve tore to the time I was in my own hospital recovery room and out of ICU, December 12, 2010, two weeks before Christmas. The next day Dr. Magovern came in to see how I was doing and I asked him when I could go home. He said his goal was to have me home by Christmas because he wanted me to be with my family. For my children, having Dad home for Christmas would be priceless.

My body had gone through such immense stress from the valve tear; it wasn't just an incision that needed to heal. My heart itself was strained, but thankfully there was no indication of heart damage. And since blood had been sucked out of my lungs multiple times over the last week, they needed time to heal. Plus, I hadn't eaten in a week and had lost more than twenty pounds. Other bodily functions needed to get working again, too. So much more needed to heal than the scar from an incision down the front of my chest.

Therapy came each day. The rehab staff performed their rehabilitation exercises with great care and concern. Amanda stayed with me most of the time, day and night. Many people from the church visited me, as well as the Bishop of the denomination, his wife, and even friends we hadn't seen in a long time. Having family and friends to love and support me through these times exponentially accelerated my recovery. It truly was a blessing from the Lord.

The Lord was answering the prayers that were going up to Heaven on my behalf. As James 5:16b says, "The prayer of a righteous man is powerful and effective." I am very thankful for all those prayers lifted up for me. The surgeon's desire for me was to be home for Christmas, but, by the end of the first week, I was ready to be discharged! I was in the hospital less than a week after my surgery and was now on my way home to my awaiting family.

The ride home was tough but well worth the trade for being able to see the faces of my five children. To be able to have Daddy back home and life becoming normal again uplifted the entire family. Of course, I couldn't pick the kids up or play with them for a while—even though I desperately wanted to—but being back at home with them was precious.

During my hospitalization, many from the church brought meals for my parents as they took care of the children. Many in the community and other churches bestowed financial gifts upon us. So many people took care of us so well that I wanted to thank as many as I could. But how could I convey that type of a "thank you"?

Every six weeks I write an article for our local newspaper's religion page, so I decided to use that space to thank the community for their prayers and support. (It seemed like the best way to get a community thank you out.) The article appeared in the January 8, 2011, issue. After explaining what had happened to me, I wrote:

During this time we have had so many praying for us. Prayer chains all around the area and country were praying. I honestly do not believe that I would have survived this if it wasn't for your prayers. God has been so good to us and the hundreds of people praying have been felt. I am very thankful for my church family at Victory Heights Church and how they have shown us unconditional love and support.

All the meals that were brought into us were appreciated. All the cards, emails, and Facebook posts showing concern have been wonderful.

The biggest thing that has blown my mind is how I have seen the love of Christ lived out in our different denominations. So often people in church (I've noticed pastors are often guilty of this) are not willing to reach out to others that do not attend "their" church, but I have experienced those walls being broken down. We have received so many gifts from churches within our community that it is getting me a little excited that we are "getting" the fact that we are working together for the Kingdom of God and not working alone.

So to all of the churches and people who have been so gracious to our family Thank You. Thank You doesn't really even convey the depth of gratitude of how we feel, but they are the only words that I can use. What I can say is that over the course of the last month I have seen the love of Christ lived in our community. Praise the Lord.

—√\\√\\√\—

The most honest and sincere reminder of this season in our lives came through our daughter Michaela. While she was in the third grade, she was assigned to write a short book on the topic of her choice. Her little book will forever impact our lives, as she wrote it shortly after my aortic valve tore.

When she wrote about our family, she highlighted some of her *Custom Scars*. What she recollects and how she feels is potent and powerful. Ultimately, I am blessed that my relationship with Amanda has stayed strong as a foundation in our lives. You can read Michaela's book in its entirety at www.customscars.org/michaelas-story.

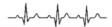

Only a few months after my second aortic valve replacement, I started to get terrible headaches at the base of the back of my head, on and off for a while, but after six months, they became a daily problem and typically very severe. It seemed that whenever the pressure changed in my head, like when I bent down to look for something under the couch, the base of my head would just pound in pain.

I went to the chiropractor, thinking this pain had something to do with my spine. I was treated the best way the chiropractor knew how, but I was typically in substantially more pain when he finished than when he started. He said the pain did not stem from anything in my spine or back, and he couldn't understand why I was having the headaches.

One day the pain was so severe I couldn't lift my head from my pillow. I took some Percocet the doctor had prescribed after my heart surgery to try to relieve the pain, but it did absolutely nothing to give me relief. That was the breaking point. I had to get to the hospital because the pain made me helpless. The local hospital wanted to transfer me via ambulance back to Allegheny General Hospital in Pittsburgh, but I didn't want to take an ambulance, so

106

Amanda drove me down. After I made my way to the ER at Allegheny General Hospital, the testing to find the cause of this pain was underway.

All my symptoms indicated a spinal fluid leak, yet neither the CT or the MRI could find such a leak. Since I was on blood thinner because of my artificial heart valve, the ER staff hesitated to do a spinal tap to check my spinal fluid pressure. With all the symptoms pointing to a spinal leak somewhere and a possible decrease in spinal fluid, the medical staff eventually agreed to perform a procedure called a blood patch.

It's a fairly easy procedure. I lay on the operating room table face down as the doctor inserted a needle into my spinal cord. Once the needle is in the correct position, blood was then quickly taken from my IV and injected into the needle in my spine. If a leak was present, my blood would then create a clot where the hole was, effectively sealing the leak. While the procedure gave me some relief, a few months later the headaches returned just as severely.

During this time it was hard to perform my duties at work. I had to lay down frequently to relieve the pressure and alleviate the pain so I could at least function a little bit.

The constant pain also took its toll on our family. I don't have much of a temper, but I developed a short fuse with my five children during this time. The physical pain simply made me say and do things I would not have under normal conditions.

In September 2012 some good friends from the church took Amanda and me to our first Pittsburgh Steelers home football game. It was the season opener and I was excited beyond words to be at Heinz Field. For some reason, during the second quarter of the game my head really started to hurt again. By the end of the game, I could hardly keep my head up because of the pressure. The trip home was almost unbearable. I felt bad for the couple who paid for our tickets and drove, as I was in pretty bad shape. I loved the home game win, but Amanda and I knew this needed to be diagnosed and treated quickly.

We scheduled an MRI and an appointment with a different neurosurgeon a month later. I was diagnosed with a Chiari 1 malformation. In essence, my brain was too big for my head. Since my brain didn't have the room it needed in my skull, the bottom lobes were being pushed into my brain stem. This also affected the flow of spinal fluid and blood around my brain, causing blurred vision, lack of balance, and substantial memory loss on top of the headaches.

In January 2013 I underwent brain surgery to relieve the pressure and pain I had been battling for more than two years. The surgeon, Dr. Baghai, felt confident either the procedure would stop the pain from getting worse or I would experience a significant improvement in all my symptomatic areas. The surgeon removed a section of my skull from the back of my head and replaced it with a patch to give my brain just a little extra room. The procedure was a success and I have been headache-free ever since.

Doctors now notice that Chiari 1 malformations are becoming more prevalent in Marfan syndrome patients even though the specific connection hasn't been pinpointed. I am not the only one with Marfan's to undergo this procedure. Future medical advancements will probably someday tell us how these two conditions are connected.

Recovery was quick and I was home three days after surgery. Once the 20+ staples were out of the back of my head, my mobility improved and I was ecstatic to be headache-free. It's incredible what a little brain surgery can do. I now have a four-inch scar on the back of my head and neck. Our youngest, who was only two, frequently climbed up to see Daddy's scar. She still rubs her fingers up and down the scar, as it is bumpy because of where the staples were.

I am exceptionally grateful for the medical advances that have prolonged my life! I do find it ironic that out of all the procedures I have ever had, brain surgery was the least painful and the quickest to recover from . . . go figure!

CUSTOM SCARS & CUSTOM CARS

At this point we have journeyed down the paths of my *Custom Scars*. I am still young, and I know I will accumulate even more scars throughout my life. Unlike my dad's 1948 Ford, I will never be completely customized until I breathe my last. Rather, God will continually, and even daily, customize me into the husband, father, friend, patient, pastor, speaker, and citizen He wants me to be.

I am glad that throughout the years my father has worked on old cars, especially his 1948 Ford Sedan. I see that car in a different light now because it doesn't look anything like an "original" or "normal" 1948 Ford would have looked more than half a century ago. Its custom builder, my father, made it exactly the way he wanted it to look and drive. He even painted it the color he wanted. Now, it is in its final customized form.

God is still customizing me and I anticipate the years ahead to see how God will use my *Custom Scars* to bring me to completion.

PROLOGUE TO TEN

This next chapter is going to be unlike any of the others. I started writing *Custom Scars* after my Chiari 1 malformation recovery in 2013. Ninety-five percent of what you just read was completed by the end of 2015, plus most of chapters eleven and twelve. I felt very strongly that my story could help people struggling with their *Custom Scars*. Our stories can hold power, help, and healing for others. I have been helped by the stories of others, and I trusted that my story could bring hope to those who feel hopeless in their lives.

After having my manuscript proofread, I submitted it to a couple acquisition editors, and even attended a three-day author's summit, but my nonfiction work made no progress of securing a publisher. I definitely learned a lot in the process and a number of people gave me terrific advice, but I was told that the book market for this genre is very crowded.

I felt defeated. I pretty much gave up and tabled the idea of publishing a book. You can purchase many other books that give hope; why would mine really even matter? Trying to be published just stopped, and I went on with my pastoral duties and family life, which are extremely time-consuming in and of themselves. Maybe this project was just for me to be able to remember the events in my life? I resigned myself to the idea that my story just wasn't good enough. That was my thinking, but God had His reason for the delay.

In the spring of 2017 I decided to reread my manuscript. I read the stories of my life and still shed many tears as I read through the pages. I read my words of the pain and sometimes hopelessness that I felt, but the unknowns and pain that were described in those first nine chapters are not even a close comparison to what our family went through in 2016.

I truly believe that my book wasn't published because one more chapter needed to be included in *Custom Scars*. Chapter ten: Dissection is going to be a chapter that is primarily written as Facebook posts. My recollection of the summer of 2016 is very scant, practically nonexistent. Amanda's updates to our family and friends will be the meat of this chapter.

I will add tidbits here and there, but this chapter is for you to be able to see the toll that a loved one's *Custom Scars* can have on a caregiver's life. It's from a different viewpoint, but I do need to say that my wife, Amanda, is extraordinary in her love for me and her love and faith in the Lord. That will be made very clear.

"Dissection" is a raw chapter that deals with immense pain. A chapter that shows how strong the human body and spirit is, but it also shows the affects that a brutal physical emergency can have on family and friends.

ten

DISSECTION

Excitement was bustling around the house on May 27, 2016, as our children had their final program for the end of another school year. The night before we had attended Jana's kindergarten graduation, and tonight was the night for the rest of the kiddos.

Typically at our house when we have an event to attend in the evening, we lose track of time. Whether it's the kids having to get their showers and then eating supper, sadly our family is known for getting there just in time. This trait comes from Amanda's side of the family (I'm sure she will love reading that), and over the last seventeen-plus years of marriage significant improvements have been made.

Supper was on the table about forty-five minutes before we needed to be at the program, and all seven of us were enjoying our meal. As I was nonchalantly enjoying my food in no real rush, Amanda abruptly said, "You still need to shower!"

I gasped. She was right, I had forgotten to shower that day. Did I even have clean clothes to wear? That really didn't matter, I just needed to finish my food, get in the shower and get clean.

We all have a pattern when we shower. Don't worry, I'm not going to share mine and I really don't need to know about yours. But when the time came for me to rinse the soap from my right armpit all I experienced was pain. Not shoulder pain, but a pain in my upper back. It wasn't a throbbing pain, but an intense pressure pain.

112

I knew immediately that I'd just had an aortic dissection. I knew that my aorta was bleeding inside of me. I knew that I was going to the hospital, if I would even survive the trip there.

I painfully got all the soap off my body and then washed my hair so I could at least be clean to go to the hospital or be clean for my casket. I knew it was a dissection, a tear in my aorta, and I didn't give myself much hope of living.

Once my sudsy body was rinsed, I could barely bend down to turn the water off and step out of the shower. I yelled for Amanda as I was staggering to try to dry off. She ran to the bathroom and I told her to get the kids in the van because I needed to get to the hospital immediately. I told her that I had a dissection.

I was only able to manage to put on a pair of mesh shorts before Amanda helped me walk to the van. The pain was extreme. My breaths were very shallow as my torso hurt to expand with each breath.

All five kids were in the van watching me writhe in pain. Michaela was fourteen, Corban was almost twelve, Dylan was ten, Andrew was seven, and little Jana was only five. I told Amanda to hurry, as I didn't have much hope I was going to survive.

We finally made it to the ER, and before I got out of the van I looked back at my five kids. Little did I know that I would only see them two times over the course of the next two months. Their eyes filled with tears and concern, I looked at them all in order to remember their faces and told them "I love you."

With tears in my eyes, I got out of the van and stumbled into the ER. I glanced at the people in the waiting room because all I had on was shorts. No shoes, no shirt, scars all over my chest. I told the receptionist that I'd just had an aortic dissection and had Marfan syndrome and that I needed to be seen immediately. I told her that time was of the essence and I needed treatment now.

I was helped by someone in the waiting room over to a wheelchair in the hallway. The receptionist then told the nurse that I was suffering back pain and it might just be kidney stones. I know what kidney stones feel like and these weren't those. Once Amanda took care of the kids I told her to sue the hospital if I died if I was treated for kidney stones instead of a dissection. Thankfully, a cardiologist from Erie was there and he heard my symptoms and the words "Marfan syndrome" and ordered a life flight for me stat.

From this point my memories are very sketchy for nearly two months, but with Amanda's help we will hopefully be able to journey from this point together.

Our local hospital did a CT scan and indeed I had a dissection but it was the best one a person could have. I had a Type B dissection where only the first two layers of my aorta had torn and not all three. The tear happened right above my upper AAA and right below the aortic arch. The pain was from the pressure of the blood going between the aortic layers.

When it was seen that it was a Type B dissection, some relief was felt, but the local doctors knew I needed to get to Allegheny General Hospital in Pittsburgh for treatment. Now starts the social media updates of our life.

May 27, 2016 ·
You never know when life will change in an instant.

Steve had a sudden extreme back pain that hasn't stopped. Those who know Marfan Syndrome know that can be very bad. We rushed him to the hospital and they life flighted him to Pittsburgh. He has had an aortic dissection. They have him stabilized and are talking options for repair tomorrow. They are keeping his blood pressure low and pain as managed as possible. We don't have definite details. Those who pray we would appreciate your prayers. God holds us all and will not leave us now. ~Amanda

May 28, 2016 ·
So as of now the Drs don't think surgery is immediately necessary. They are controlling his blood pressure and trying to manage the pain. They believe since the tear was on the inside wall of his aorta that it should heal on its own. Long term something could be done down the road but for now just healing. Thank you all who are praying! We can't express our thanks enough.

God is good!!!! He cares about us all. ~Amanda

May 29, 2016 ·
Steve update: I don't have much information. Steve isn't improving in the ways the Drs had hoped. They are discussing surgery again. There are so many unknowns but I wanted to keep everyone informed.

God gives strength to the weak and weary. ~Amanda

May 29, 2016 ·
Steve's oxygen levels dropped today. Partially due to fluid retention and partially due to his pain levels making him not want to take deep breaths. They have switched up some of his medication, including his pain meds, and put him on a BiPap machine to assist him in taking deeper breaths. He seems more settled tonight then when I got in with him this morning.

They are still discussing letting him heal -vs- procedure -vs- full blown surgery. The surgeon that saw him tonight was going to email all his scans to the lead vascular surgeon to get his opinion.

God never leaves us or forsakes us. ~Amanda

May 31, 2016 ·
Steve update:
I've tried to start this update so many times. It is hard to explain everything and there still is so much we don't know. I'll do my best and please excuse my grammatical errors and rambling. I know it is important to get the info out so people know how to pray and because so many of you want to know about Steve. So I'll do my best.

For reasons we aren't entirely sure of on Sunday, or Saturday night after I left, Steve started having a difficult time breathing and catching his breath. The doctors ultimately had to start him on a BiPap machine to push more air in his lungs when

115

he breathes. They feel it is because he is retaining fluid so they are working to correct that still.

Please pray for wisdom for the Drs. We are still waiting on a final word if we need to do a surgery or not. At this point they have to get him breathing better first if that is the way to go. This tear in his aorta caused a 5cm aneurysm but they usually don't operate until 6cm but Steve is more complicated than most. A gradual growth of a 5cm aneurysm is different than an aneurysm that is the result of a tear too.

We appreciate all those who are praying for us and the offers of help. We are just going day by day and relying on God to care for us. I read this yesterday and loved it so much I wanted to share:

Psalm 62:5 "Find rest, O my soul, in God alone; my hope comes from Him. He alone is my rock and my salvation; He is my fortress, I will not be shaken."

I pray you all know that Giver of hope. If not, please find Jesus today. You never know when your life may change in an instant. ~Amanda

June 1, 2016 ·
Steve's breathing became such an issue last night they had to put him on a ventilator. I haven't been able to be back to see him yet this morning because they are doing a procedure on another patient in the SICU. Please continue praying that his lungs will clear. And if there is another issue causing his breathing issues they will find it. Thanks to everyone for their support and prayers. I can't reply to all the messages and notes just know I read them.

Trusting in God, my Giver of hope ~Amanda

June 1, 2016 ·
Not much has changed since this morning. Steve has been sedated and has a breathing tube. He is still retaining fluid. I don't know what the Drs have decided or if they are still discussing. I know Steve's past history of 4 heart/aneurysm surgeries truly complicates things. I'm just constantly praying for wisdom for the Drs as they make some tough calls. Only God knows the future and I am trusting in His will.

This verse was shared with me today and I love it.

"For I hold you by your right hand— I, the LORD your God. And I say to you, 'Don't be afraid. I am here to help you. (Isaiah 41:13 NLT). ~Amanda

June 2, 2016 · Post from our friend Barbara
Just letting you know I prayed for Steve several times today. Every time his name came to mind I prayed. Thank you for showing your strength and faith to all of us. I truly hope today was a better day.

June 2, 2016 ·
I saw the Critical Care Dr on the floor today. The Dr said that they have found an infection in Steve's lungs. They are running cultures to see which antibiotic he needs. He is pretty stable but the Dr wants to have his lungs dry out before he

116

would pull him off the ventilator. The Dr believes that is what has caused his breathing issues.

A Vascular resident came and talked to me. She said that the lung issue isn't connected to his aorta issue at all. She feels once his breathing is better that he will be able to go home as they had planned.

He is still sedated and on a ventilator. Thank you all for your support.
~Amanda

Psalm 121:1-2 NIV
[1] I lift up my eyes to the mountains---where does my help come from? [2] My help comes from the Lord, the Maker of heaven and earth.

June 4, 2016 ·
Yesterday not much had changed with Steve so I didn't write an update as I was very tired at 10 when I left his room.

The Drs were saying it is pneumonia, the kind of pneumonia they aren't sure. They are still testing to find which strain of pneumonia to find the right antibiotic to fight it. I'm continuing to pray for wisdom for the Drs and nursing staff so they can get Steve on the road to recovery.

This morning as I was reading my Bible I came across the account of Solomon and the building of the temple. I figured that since we are now the temple of God it would apply today as well. This was my prayer this morning for Steve and those around him. ~Amanda

2 Chronicles 6:19 "Yet give attention to your servant's prayer and his plea for mercy, O Lord my God. Hear the cry and the prayer that your servant is praying in your presence."

June 4, 2016 · Post from our friend Dave (Same Dave who dropped me on my head)
Lord, Today is Saturday and I can only imagine how much both Steve and Amanda would love to be home. I know from my own experience that Saturday is a time to get caught up on life and spend time with family. Please touch Steve right now may they have a very keen awareness of your presence. Help the doctors to be able to find out what is best for his infection and how best to get him home. Help Amanda as she is having to make grown up decisions that she is facing. Keep her face in your face. Let Your faithfulness be overwhelming present. Be with the kids. Help them to have fun in their lives. May they miss Mom n dad... enough to bring joy to their parents heart but not to the burdening. Help those who are carrying for them to help some fun memories during this time. Draw them close to each other and closer to Yourself.

Amen

June 5, 2016 ·
Yesterday Steve was much the same as before. The Dr said his lungs weren't any worse but weren't any better. I'll take that as good because at least they weren't worse. Steve did develop a low grade fever toward evening and they had to bump

117

up some things on his ventilator to keep his oxygen up. I don't claim to know everything medically but I am just praying that God will speak to the medical staff and just give them the wisdom to the best courses of action. God made Steve and knows exactly what needs done. We will rest in that knowledge.

I hope you all have a good Sunday in church worshipping a God who saves and loves His people. If you don't go to a church, why not start now. You never know when life will change in an instant. ~Amanda

June 6, 2016 · Post from a friend Laura
Tonight Carly was wondering about her skin and what was under it and we talked about How amazing God is that He knows just how to make us. So we started talking about Pastor Steve and how God knows just what he needs. After we prayed for him Carly asked me if he was going to get a sticker at the hospital. I told her I didn't know so she insisted on sending him a purple one (her favorite color). Love you guys!

June 7, 2016 · (One week on ventilator)
Steve still remains in the ICU. His lungs are the issue now. The Cardio-thoracic Dr said that he truly believes the aortic dissection(tear) can be medically managed until it reaches a point that calls for surgery. The dissection and pneumonia aren't connected which he very clearly and patiently explained to me. I'll save you all the details. He feels that Steve picked up pneumonia along the way. Whether he brought the pneumonia from home, picked it up at the hospital, or just from laying in bed it doesn't matter. We need to beat it either way.

His lungs seem worse to me about everyday except yesterday. The critical care dr did a procedure Sunday night to take samples from his lungs and he said we are testing for EVERYTHING. Every virus or bacteria will be tested. So far the cultures haven't grown anything but it can take days or weeks depending on the cause. This Dr wants answers just as bad as we do and I think he takes it a little personally that he doesn't have a final answer yet so he is truly searching for answers.

Steve is still mostly sedated which is best for him. Being on a ventilator is not a pleasant experience. Thank you for all the support and encouragement you all have sent our way. I've read so many messages that just show how great our God is. We are storming the gates of heaven sharing our requests for Steve's healing.

God will take care of us. I just trust and lean on Him. He truly holds our future in His hands. ~Amanda

June 9, 2016 · (This is our 15 year Wedding Anniversary)
Steve remains in the ICU on the ventilator. His oxygen numbers have slowly been rising while the Drs are able to ever so slowly turn down some settings on his ventilator. The Dr said while he is slowly getting better we have a very long road ahead of us. Steve's lungs are very sick and will take time to heal. Earlier in the week we were beginning to discuss if we were going to need to put him on a

machine to artificially oxygenate his blood. Today we are able to table that and stay the course with a ventilator.

Steve developed a fever again yesterday. They are going to change up his antibiotics a little today. He isn't fully sedated anymore but still very unaware because of all the meds.

God will make a way and I put all my trust in Him. ~Amanda

June 10, 2016 ·
Steve's lungs are definitely starting to improve. His oxygen is up and they did turn down levels on his ventilator last night and he is still holding strong.

But remember how the Dr said this will be a long road? While his lungs are improving we have a new situation. He started passing blood today. He is on a Heparin iv, due to his mechanical valve, and that doesn't help matters. They ended up giving him a blood transfusion this afternoon while they look for the source. Also, he still has a fever that comes and goes. Steve is still unaware of all of this because of all the pain meds please keep praying.

I know we will make it through. I received this verse on a card today. It is a definite encouragement. James 4:8 "Draw near to God and He will draw near to you." ~Amanda

June 13, 2016 ·
Steve's lungs are still improving. Yesterday they turned the settings on the ventilator to allow him to breath on his own and he did great! Because he has been on the ventilator so long he did wear out toward nighttime and so they switched the ventilator back to assisting him more over night to give his body a rest. We will probably go back and forth through these settings quite often until he is stronger. It's just like exercising a muscle you haven't used in awhile. You have to workout it and rest it until it is in shape.

They are also doing a scope this morning to try and find the source of his bleeding. The bleeding has almost stopped but they haven't fed him anything since it started. I'm hoping and praying that will be an easy fix so we don't set back the progress we are making. Hopefully, we will have answers on that soon.

They turned off Steve's sedation yesterday too. He wasn't really awake yet because of the amount in his system. Bad thing is they have to sedate him again to do the scope but we are hoping to allow him to fully be awake in the next few days. It's a slow road with a lot of waiting but progress is progress.

Thank you for your continued prayers and support. I've just been learning patience and to trust God. ~Amanda

June 13, 2016 ·
After I posted this morning I went in to see Steve and he had a bit of a setback. The bleeding had started again and was actually pretty bad. The Dr went ahead and did the scope this afternoon. He found an ulcer in his small intestines (not 3 ulcers, sorry family on my confusion earlier in the text I sent) which he clamped 3 times. He wanted to make sure it doesn't come apart again before it

heals but it actually was on the smaller side. The ulcer should heal and the clamps will then fall off. No procedure necessary for that part.

His breathing has been excellent and his oxygen levels high. They only changed his ventilator off of CPap because of doing a scope.

All of this is good news to me as I see Steve making more progress toward healing. Sometimes it is two steps forward and one step back. I'm trusting in God to care for all of us. After all, what good is my faith if I turn away now. I know God sees us and cares. It may not make sense to me at times but He sees the big picture.

Have a blessed Monday. After all, isn't it great to be alive. ~Amanda

June 15, 2016 ·
I just walked in with Steve. He was pretty stable yesterday. Apparently early this morning he started bleeding again. They are going to do another scope. He is losing a lot of blood at the moment. I'd appreciate prayers. I know you've been praying. ~Amanda

June 15, 2016 ·
Steve is stabilized. They gave him 4 units of blood this morning. His numbers are leveling out now.

They did the scope and felt that the bleeding was coming from the ulcer they had clamped earlier. It has almost totally stopped bleeding, if not completely stopped. They changed some of his medications and stopped the Heparin (blood thinner) for now. The Drs may do a colonoscopy tomorrow to make sure there isn't another source of bleeding.

Thank you everyone for praying. I wasn't sure Steve was going to pull through this time. But God is good and heard our prayers. Blessed be the name of The Lord. ~Amanda

June 17, 2016 · (17 days on ventilator)
Praise God! So far Steve's bleeding has stopped! His lungs have greatly improved! They would like to take him off of the ventilator today or tomorrow. He is coughing and fighting the tube but if he will relax and just breathe they will better be able to assess the true condition of his lungs. He actually can get so worked up he will make himself vomit. But really, who wouldn't with a plastic tube in your throat.

So Steve's job for today is to relax and take long, deep breaths. God is so good! ~Amanda

June 18, 2016 ·
I would love to tell you all that Steve was off the ventilator but he isn't. Everything else seems to be progressing nicely. His nurse said today, "It's like running a marathon. His lungs have to work and rest until they are strong because once the race starts there is no turning back."

120

The Dr said he is right there but not quite ready. They feel confident that very soon they can take out the ventilator. Then the next step begins.

Thank you all for praying for us. Wednesday was so difficult but I know the power of prayer to a God who hears can change anything. ~Amanda

June 19, 2016 · (Day 19 and it's out)
This will be a short post.
Steve is off the ventilator!!!! Praise God!
He is breathing great!!! I thought you would want to know. ~Amanda

June 19, 2016 ·
I heard one the best things ever today. When leaving Steve's room tonight he whispered, "I love you too."

I wasn't sure last week if I'd ever hear that again. It's been at least three weeks since I have. Still an uphill battle for Steve to recover but at least he is making good progress. Resting in God's peace tonight. ~Amanda

(some replies to post)

Vicki - I can't stop smiling! So happy to know you can hear his voice again, especially those words! God is SO good!

Mark - Praying for his full recovery

Barb - Happy tears....the things we should not take for granted, ever!

Ruth Ann (my aunt) - Many Happy Tears! Love You

Josh - Very thankful for his progress and God's answer to prayer. Thanks for all the updates. We will keep praying.

Dr. John - Thankful. Praying nonstop.

Pat - Thankful tears of joy. Keeping you both in my prayers.

Cheryl - Such wonderful words for you to hear.

Julie - 10,000 Reasons for my heart to sing... This is one of them. So very thankful that you got to hear that again.

Alison - Made me tear up...sometimes hearing those words at this time is the BEST medicine! God IS good!

Sara - How very wonderful...So happy I started to cry.

Lisa - Amanda, I am so thankful you got that...still praying!

Chad - God is Good

Pam - AWESOME !!!!!!

Connie - Glad to hear praying for full recovery

Amelia - Amazing!

Laura - Yay!!!

Sandy - My heart is warmed, Praise God!

Barbara - This makes me want to scream Hallelujah Praise God!! Amanda your faith has been such a stronghold.

Carol - Three of the most powerful words there is. Praise the Lord for answer to prayers. He is an amazing God!!!

121

June 21, 2016 ·

Steve has been breathing fine, maybe a little fast. His lungs still need to continue to heal.

Steve is so weak. Physical therapy was here yesterday and helped him sit on the side of the bed. The goal was a chair but he wasn't able to stay sitting on his own.

The sedation was really clearing out of his mind last night and he had many questions. The main one, how did I get to this point? He can't fully talk yet so it was a whispered questioned. I'm still praying for continued healing and strength. Steve has a long road to recovery. I'm not sure what all we are looking at.

Thank you for all your prayers and support. Since Steve is awake more I'm not sure how many updates I will continue to have time for. I'm praising God for His healing touch. ~Amanda

June 22, 2016 ·

I remembered many would be at church tonight and people would want to know. I just found out more details.

This morning Steve started to have severe pain again. They did another CT scan this morning and unfortunately the tear has gotten worse. Nothing is leaking but it did expand. The surgeon does not feel comfortable sending him home like that. He originally planned to do that so Steve could come into surgery healthy. We were talking rehab facilities this morning.

The surgeon would prefer to do an open surgery through the side but he doesn't feel Steve is strong enough for that. He plans to do an endograph (go through the groin up to the dissection and then open up a graft from the inside to cover/seal the tear) toward the end of the week after he studies all of Steve's scans.

I had an encouraging visit this morning and I was reminded how none of this surprises God. And I keep remembering how God holds us in the palm of His hand. I will continue to trust Him and rest in His promises. There is no one I trust more. ~Amanda

June 24, 2016 ·

Steve's surgery will be at 6:45 Friday morning, 6/24. He told his surgeon that thousands are praying for him. His surgeon said we will take all the help we can get. ~Amanda

June 24, 2016 ·

Steve's surgery went perfectly according to his surgeon. He said it wasn't easy because of Steve's age and Marfan Syndrome but everything was according to plan procedure wise. Steve's blood was thinner than they like for doing a surgery but the surgeon felt that we couldn't wait any longer. Steve was experiencing quite a bit of pain through the night and it just wasn't worth the risk to wait any longer.

Now he is again on the ventilator and will be for today at least. With the lung issues he has been having they want to play it safe. The surgeon said we don't want him to be working to breathe right now.

122

They did want to do a spinal tap before the procedure to help with blood flow to the spine and to reduce the risk of paralysis. Steve's INR (blood thinner level) was too high for that so as they can get those levels down they will complete that procedure.

Praise be to God for His unfailing mercy and strength. I would never be able to make this journey without Him. Thank you all who have before bringing us before God. Our God is an awesome God. ~Amanda

June 24, 2016 ·

Update: the Drs came out a little bit ago and told me Steve was passing blood again. He was able to do a scope again and cauterize yet another ulcer. He said to pray that is it because he can't keep doing the cauterizations or there is the risk of perforating the bowel. Steve is stable again.

When a Dr tells me to pray I do and wanted to share with others. Other than this new bleeding episode everything else is going great. ~Amanda

June 26, 2016 · (Only on ventilator for 2 days)

So huge praise!!!!! Steve is off the ventilator!!!!!! Again! This time it went very smoothly and quickly. His breathing and oxygen numbers are great and he seems more like himself than he has since this started.

We keep praying that the bleeding ulcers don't come back or for any new ones to start. His nurse last night said because of the location of them you can tell it is from the physical stress his body had been on with this tear. (Different than emotional stress like work, moving, etc.)

I'm not going to be here tomorrow because it is Jana's 6th birthday and those that know Jana know how important her birthday is to her. Steve's parents will be here with him part of the day so he isn't alone. Please pray for them and him because he doesn't do well without me. When he asked what time I was coming in tomorrow I told him I wasn't coming and why. He said, "Skip it."

Hopefully we are fully on the road to recovery now. Thanks again for all the prayers and support. We will never be able to thank you all. Have a blessed Sunday. ~Amanda

June 28, 2016 ·

I am so excited!!!! Steve was greatly improved when I saw him today. Not himself yet but a lot better than Sunday.

It seems Steve's anxiety issue has passed as far as I can tell for now. But really, who wouldn't be stir crazy after being in the ICU for a month.

They have him in a chair doing "therapy" as much as he can stay awake. Stacking cans, folding washcloths, and working on swallowing to strengthen his throat. The speech therapist said he is definitely swallowing but isn't getting the flap completely sealed over his windpipe to the lungs to keep the liquids out of the lungs. She gave him a list of exercises to strengthen his throat muscles.

They started his Heparin IV again because we need him on blood thinner so the artificial heart valve he has doesn't have a clot form. That would cause a whole

123

new set of issues. Please pray he doesn't end up with any new bleeding ulcers. His Heparin has made those an issue.

It seems we are on the road to recovery. Praise the Lord!!! I'm going to post a song that has really meant a lot to me on this journey. It's called Thy Will and it is truly my hearts cry. May you put your trust in God as well if you haven't already. ~Amanda

June 30, 2016 ·

So much has happened in just a few days. And so far, all of it good things.

Steve was able to stand today for the first time! He had quite a bit of help from physical therapy getting up but he stood for 55 seconds! Rehab is definitely in our future but he is making such good progress everyone is pleased.

Also, today is the day we leave ICU!!!!!!! They are moving him to a step down room across the hall. It is one day shy of 5 weeks in the ICU. He will remain here until he is medically stable. Meaning we have to have his medications figured out and all test results come back correctly to be certain everything is stable. Then he will move to rehab where the focus is in physical and occupational therapy to get his strength back.

Thank you again for all your prayers and support. There were days where I wasn't sure Steve would make it. I know God heard our prayers and answered in healing and helping Steve. Steve even told me last night he should've been dead. God was and is gracious and merciful in sparing one we love so much. It doesn't always end this way but I will praise God either way. This time it is easy. ~Amanda

July 2, 2016 ·

Steve has been doing amazing. Yesterday and today when physical therapy was in he was able to scoot off the bed into a chair. Medically he seems really stable and honestly if this wasn't a holiday weekend he would probably be at rehab today or tomorrow. As it stands now we will be moving him there on Tuesday as long as nothing changes between now and then.

Which brings me to the decision of where to send him. We have a Transitional Care Unit at the local hospital and there is also a rehab facility down here in Pittsburgh. We have to decide where he needs to go. He'd like to be close to home but prior to his surgery I didn't feel comfortable with him being almost 2 hours away from the hospital in case the tear worsened. Now the tear is fixed so that makes a local rehab more of a possibility. Decisions, decisions, decisions......something I'm terrible at. Also, we need to decide if we should still move houses. (Some of you knew we were planning on moving closer to the church.) Pretty much all that is left to do is sign papers, and pack, and move, and paint, and unpack, and sell our current house.

Thanks again for your prayers and support. I love when I see the church come around those who need support and to watch the power of God. I am again humbled by it all. ~Amanda

124

July 4, 2016 ·
Happy 4th of July everyone! I love a holiday and celebrating America is always fun. I hope you are all able to do that in some way.

Steve has been doing really well over the weekend. We are still having ups and downs, especially with confusion, but more good days than bad. It's so nice to be able to chat again even if he dozes off frequently. I still can't believe the journey we have been on this last month. God's blessings are never ending and His love unfailing.

Have a happy 4th and maybe hug your loved ones a little closer. You never know when it could all change in an instant. ~Amanda

July 6, 2016 ·
We are finally at TCU (Transitional Care Unit) 5 minutes from our house. What a blessing. The staff are so caring already. ~Amanda

July 6, 2016 ·
I don't know why a girl who can find her way around a 13 floor hospital in Pittsburgh with her eyes closed can't seem to find her way around a 1 floor transitional unit. Lol! ~Amanda

July 7, 2016 ·
(Steve posting) Gonna be weeks of rehab but day I I know I I am loved. Please no calls or visits as I need to focus on me getting better. Thanks.

July 7, 2016 ·
Got the shakes. Please pray. These are hard to handle. Steve.

I'm going to break into the story here for a little bit. I think you can agree that I have an absolutely incredible wife. Her story is mind-blowing!

I honestly don't have any significant memories of any of the updates that Amanda or I wrote. I was so sedated and sick that I am very glad that those memories are lost. But I do have some memories when I was moved closer to home to our Transitional Care Unit (TCU) in Seneca, PA.

The transport trip up from Allegheny General Hospital was about an hour and a half. The summer of 2016 was brutally hot and the transport vehicle I rode from Allegheny General Hospital to the

Transitional Care Unit's air conditioning wasn't working correctly. The temperature that day was in the low nineties and the ninety-plus mile trip was absolutely brutal. Soaked in sweat and not feeling well at all, I was so pleased to pull into a familiar setting not far from home. Sadly, my stay was only going to be for two days.

Early in the morning on July 8, I had a dream. It was a dream that the devil was literally telling me how worthless I was and how physically frail I had become over these last six to seven weeks. At this point I was in bad shape, struggling to even feed myself. I couldn't walk, my arms were so weak, and I didn't even have the strength to put my legs over the side of the bed to even try to sit up, so Satan had some good fodder for his accusations. But then it got worse.

In this weakened state I still didn't have any type of good bowel control, and sadly, I made a terrible mess that second night in TCU. Satan again berated me on how pitiful I was and that they were going to throw me out of the facility because of the mess I had made. I felt so bad to have to call for help, but I couldn't even roll out of my own waste.

I finally woke up, or came to my right mind, and proceeded to call for an aide. I started to cry when she came in to clean me up. I felt terrible causing this mess and apologized profusely. The aide was very gracious, cleaned me up, and back to sleep I went. Before Amanda made it in that morning, I had another BM and was practically carried out of bed to get on the toilet seat beside me. By the time I was helped back into the bed, I was completely exhausted.

I hadn't been back in my bed for long when Amanda arrived at TCU. Within a couple minutes of her arrival I needed to use the toilet again. When I was lifted up, I almost passed out. I was quickly lowered back into bed in order not to fall over. Through some other observations it was realized that my ulcers had started to bleed again and I had lost a substantial amount blood.

After over six attempts to find a vein, one was finally found strong enough to start the blood transfusion. I was in such bad shape that they actually had two infusions running at the same time to get blood back into me at a more rapid rate. The life flight was called and back to Pittsburgh I was flown.

It was so hot outside heading to the helicopter, but I was freezing cold due to blood loss. Who knows how many pints of blood I had lost. They wrapped me in a shiny space blanket and for the entire flight down the medics didn't turn the air conditioning on in the chopper. These guys were sweating profusely in order to help me stay warm. They made conversation with me the entire trip to keep me awake and did a great job taking care of me.

Once back down in Pittsburgh, another half dozen units of blood were needed and other options about my care were to be considered.

July 8, 2016 ·
Please pray for Steve. He is bleeding again. They are going to get him back down to Pittsburgh but he really needs prayer. Thank you. ~Amanda

July 8, 2016 ·
We are back in Pittsburgh. Steve is in the ICU again. He is stable and they are watching him closely. They gave him 2 units of blood before he even got down here. There will be more testing tomorrow. I don't know much more than that right now.
Steve shared his favorite verse with a therapist earlier today. My grace is sufficient for you. My strength is made perfect in your weakness. 2 Corinthians 10 I believe. Not an exact quote but exactly what I needed for this evening. ~Amanda

July 9, 2016 ·
The Drs did a scope again and the bleeding ulcer that has been fixed/cauterized previously was bleeding again. They Dr was able to clip it but they said if it starts again there will need to be a surgery to fix it.

Thank you for all your prayers. Steve is awake and thinking clearly. He is hoping to heal up his stomach and eat again soon. God is good! ~Amanda

July 10, 2016 · (Steve's post)
Given more blood this morning. Tough night

July 10, 2016 ·
Today was thankfully a peaceful day. Steve is doing well and his vital signs are stable. They have given him blood again today. They are still trying to get his blood levels where they belong.

They plan to do a surgery tomorrow to go in and somehow clip or cut off the artery that is bleeding. It will be through his leg again and if this takes care of the problem bleed we will be on the road to recovery. If not they will have to do an open surgery the next day and go in to sew off the artery. We do not have a time of day for this but I wanted to let everyone know what is going on with Steve. He seems to be thinking very clearly if not a little restless. Thank you all for your prayers through this roller coaster ride. God is in control. ~Amanda

July 11, 2016 ·
Slept better. Hopefully having bleeding spot in belly surgically fixed this morning. Please pray. Steve.

July 11, 2016 · Post from a friend – Stephen
God, bring a complete and total Healing to Steve! Through the blood of Jesus and stripes he bore for us, We claim Steve's healing right now.

July 11, 2016 ·
Still waiting..... No definitive time for surgery yet. ~Amanda

July 11, 2016 ·
So, unfortunately, they aren't doing the surgery. The surgeon feels because Steve is no longer "actively bleeding" they won't be able to be sure to stop the correct artery. The clamp seems to be holding from Saturday so we are back to the waiting game. If it bleeds they will rush him in. If not we just pray it heals.

To say I am frustrated is an understatement. I understand why they made the decision but that doesn't make it any easier. Steve said we need to specifically pray that nothing breaks open again and that his ulcer completely heals up. We will continue to trust in God and His will. ~Amanda

July 11, 2016 · (Steve's post)
They didn't do surgery. We need focused prayer that nothing tears in my stomach ever again and there is complete healing. I will be in hospital for a while. Pray for kids too.

July 13, 2016 ·
Ate too much for lunch and aggravated the ulcer. Hurt so bad. We don't think it tore again I just have to slow down eating
Please continue to pray for complete healing, no bleeding, and that I can sleep tonight. Long road but slowly moving forward
Was able to shuffle a few steps with help but I can stand for about 10 seconds. So that's progress
Back pain is still strong appreciate prayer for that.
Steve

July 14, 2016 ·
I'm gonna try to breakdown what's going on
I'm heading to a rehab center down here to get stronger and walking again the reason I'll be here is because if my ulcer bleeds again I am able to be near AGH.
I have been taken off my blood thinner for my heart valve too try to encourage a quicker healing of the ulcer
This is high risk because of blood clots. I'm stuck between a rock and a hard place.
Pray for no clots, causing a stroke, and that the ulcer heals completely
I'll be off my blood thinner for two weeks. It's all very touchy. I'll have a scope in two weeks to see if ulcer is healed. If so I will then go back on blood thinner. - Steve

July 15, 2016 · (Steve's post)
At transitional care. Will start more consistent rehab tomorrow. PTL that I can stand with help and stay standing for about10 seconds fairly steady. Months to go but it's a start.

July 16, 2016 ·
It's gonna be aggressive rehab but today I stood with a walker for one minute. Exhausting to stand that long but progress will be intense
Continue to pray for no stomach bleeds or blood clots. If I don't experience either of those I think I'll make it. -Steve

July 16, 2016 ·
Need prayer. Having some emotional stress. Steve

July 17, 2016 ·

I haven't posted for awhile. Steve has been doing a good job at that. I just thought I would give everyone a basic update on what is going on now.

As many of you know we headed back down here to Pittsburgh on the 8th because Steve was having another bleeding episode with his stomach ulcer. Long story short, they clamped it again and have had him off his blood thinner since then trying to get his ulcer to fully heal.

Last Thursday evening the 14th, late evening, he was transferred to a rehab facility still down here in Pittsburgh to begin more intense physical therapy to regain his strength. The Drs and us wanted him close to his main hospital just in case he would have any complications of the GI bleed or of not being on blood thinner with a mechanical valve.

Since Steve has been here he has made great progress physically. He can stand almost fully by himself with a nurse or aid right there if help is needed. Then with help steve can "dance" a shuffling few steps to turn and sit in the chair. Such progress from even a week ago!

I think we need to continue to pray for the ulcer to heal, to pray that he will not have any blood clots on his mechanical valve, and most of all to pray for his anxiety and discouragement. I am going home tonight for a few days and it is really difficult for Steve to think about being without me. He understands why I am needed at home but that doesn't make it easy. As he gets better it also sometimes is more difficult for him to not be able to get up and walk around.

We thank you all again for your prayers and support on this crazy, long journey. The church had joined together and reminded us how God intended us to support each other through trials. Psalm 107 has meant a lot to me and I wanted to share it and remind everyone what a mighty God we serve. Psalm 107:6 "Then they cried out to The Lord in their trouble, and He delivered them from their distress." This is written in this Psalm three times. Apparently God knew we needed to be reminded more than once that He will deliver us. ~Amanda

P.S. I'll probably leave most of the updating up to Steve as I'm not going to be with him everyday now. And also because I am going to be focusing a lot on our move to a different house in our area. That is a situation that was begun months ago and we were initially going to close on our new house May 27th, the day so much changed in an instant.

July 18, 2016 ·

Had my first full day of rehab. 50 minutes PT and 50 minutes OT. Exhausted. One and two pound weights wiped me out.

It's intense but that's how you get better. Stood a little longer today too. Hopefully by next week some steps will be in an update. Your prayers and support for our family have been so appreciated. - Steve

July 19, 2016 ·

Another day of therapy. Pretty sore but it's amazing what each day you can achieve. Walked (shuffled) with a walker today about ten feet forward. Major success.

Had two pastors from up home visit and that was nice too

My step brother, Ron, who had a kidney transplant last week called and encouraged me to press on. That call made my day. He's doing good too.

My parents are coming down tomorrow so I'm looking forward to that.

Other details about my ulcer it sounds like they may look at it at the end of next week when I'm stronger. (Actually they just told me it will be next Wednesday they will see how the ulcer is) Still pray that it heals completely and that no blood clots occur since I'm off my blood thinner.

Love you all

Steve

July 20, 2016 ·

Very tired this evening. Pushed hard in PT today. Walked 80 feet. My leg muscles are tight but it was a significant accomplishment. Not going to be able to do as much tomorrow unless legs recoup well tonight.

My parents came down for a visit which was nice too as they brought more of my clothes down.

I think I am going to attempt to shave tomorrow. You can pray that I have the strength too. I get really tired just brushing my teeth and hair so it will be a big accomplishment.

No bleeding so that's good too.

Thank you again for your prayers. Those are what have sustained me and my family.

July 21, 2016 ·

The day went pretty well. Painful PT session but my muscles are really tight. Looking forward to Amanda coming down Saturday. I miss her so much.

One day at a time. It can be hard but it's just one day at a time.

July 22, 2016 ·

Stomach hasn't felt the best today. I think it's because I'm so excited that Amanda is coming tomorrow.

Good PT and OT. Legs are sore but walked about 50 feet today.

The biggest prayer concern is that my stomach scope next Wednesday comes back with the ulcer 100% healed.

Again, your prayers and support for our family through this time has been a blessing to our family.

July 23, 2016 ·

I could use a transporter from Star Trek right about now. I'm heading back down to Pittsburgh to see Steve again and wishing it didn't take so long to drive it. ~Amanda

July 23, 2016 ·

Got my hair cut and I am wiped out. Only had PT today and it was early this morning. Good friends John and Beth came for a visit which was nice. Amanda's here and she's going to sleep in the chair beside me tonight.

That's about it for today

July 24, 2016 ·

Ended up with a debilitating headache today. Pretty much all afternoon was in major pain. Tramadol plus extra strength Tylenol and a 30 minute nap took care of it.

Amanda headed home about 30 minutes ago. It was nice to have her here this weekend. My parents came down too today but it was during the throes of my headache so I didn't visit with them well.

Feel really good tonight and going to try to sleep without taking pain killer or sleeping aid.

Wednesday's coming for my scope. Please continue to pray all is healed ulcer wise.

July 25, 2016 · From a friend Tracy:

StephenandAmanda Henry, we continue to pray for you all and mostly for your healing! We all love you. Every Monday here at school, our prayer group meets and you are on that list for prayer as well. Our church has also been praying continually for you. God is good and I'm happy to hear your headache got taken care of!

"But this I call to mind and therefore I have hope; The steadfast love of the LORD never ceases; his mercies never come to an end; they are new every morning; great is your faithfulness. The LORD is my portion" says my soul, "therefore I will hope in him." Lamentations 3:21-25

July 25, 2016 ·

I ended up having OT and PT back to back today. Made it a little more tiring today. Didn't eat well for breakfast or lunch but ate all my supper and just had potato chips and crackers.

Walked about 80 feet today and they are very pleased with my progress.

On another note we closed on our new house today. It's gonna take a little work but at least we can get in now. It's closer to the church with more room. Our current house needs to sell now. Pray for Amanda because I will be of no help in this move.

Love you all and thank you for your prayers and support.

Steve

July 26, 2016 ·
Had a good day today. Haven't taken any pain meds and feel pretty good. I'm not allowed to eat or drink anything after midnight tonight as I have a stomach scope scheduled for 11AM to see if the ulcer is healed. Please pray that all is completely healed so I can get back on my blood thinner.

Amanda will be driving down in the morning to be with me as I'll go to AGH for the scope.

I'm trying to figure snacks this evening in order to be full late tonight and maybe wouldn't be as hungry in the morning.

Walked about 100 feet, did some leg lifts, a couple of squats, and a couple toe lifts.

The open sore on the base of my tailbone is healing well too.

Still don't have a timeframe for when I can go home but it would be so nice if it can be by mid August and have home therapy and then go to our local therapy facility.

The beginning of my path home is significantly based off of what is found tomorrow. That's why prayers are so important right now.

Thank you all - Steve.

July 27, 2016 ·
Steve had his scope done today to check on his bleeding ulcer. Praise The Lord it is totally healed!!!!!!! There is a scar where it was and a couple spots of inflammation but everything is healed. He will restart his blood thinner tonight. Thank you for all your prayers and support. We are one step closer to recovery.

God is good! ~Amanda

July 27, 2016 ·
Amanda updated a few hours ago but we found out today that they are planning on discharging me to go HOME next Thursday.

So much needs to be done in order for our new house to be ready in 8 days. Another FB post will be coming but I believe that a clean and paint work day is being scheduled for this Saturday. Like I said more info is coming.

It's been exactly two months since my aortic dissection when I was knockin' on Heavens door, but will be very glad to get home.

It's actually surreal to think about coming home so please pray for me and my anxiousness. I am wiped out right now but Amanda is going to get me a sub sandwich so hopefully that will give me some strength.

Love you all, Steve

July 28, 2016 ·
Good rehab today. Going to be starting my Coumadin tonight. Lousy thing is I just had my first lovenox shot in my belly. I have to have them twice a day and they hurt.

Good thing is that I'll be coagulated soon and blood clot risk will be removed. One week from today and hopefully I'll be on my way home.

July 28, 2016 ·

Accomplished a first tonight. Some of you may find this gross, but I was able to use my walker to get into the restroom to use it. Two months since I've done that. Tiring, but if I'm going home next week, I got to do it. Big and exhausting accomplishment - Steve

July 28, 2016 ·

Yuck, another lovenox shot in the belly. Going to sleep soon. Could use prayers for a good nights sleep. Last night I stopped taking a sleeping aid pill and tonight's the same. Goodnight.

July 29, 2016 ·

It's that time again. Had good rehab sessions today. Practiced stepping into a bathtub and using a cane. Surpassing therapy's goals. Since tomorrow is a work day at our new house Amanda isn't coming down for the weekend. That makes me sad.

If you're in the area and can give a hand tomorrow that would be great. The more help the better.

Bad thing is I fell asleep for about 20 minutes at 7pm. I hope I can sleep fine tonight. Last night I didn't sleep well because of vivid dreams.

Waiting for my lovenox shot and then it is tv watching and snacking.

Goodnight

Steve

July 30, 2016 ·

I had a different person for PT today as it's the weekend. She just wanted me to walk for endurance but I have to be careful not to overdue it. After my third 100 foot walk my blood pressure and heart rate tanked. I've typically been 120 bpm and it dropped to the 60's. That ended pt then. Things got back to normal in about an hour.

My blood is thinning slowly. My INR is 1.3 and once I hit 2.0 I will be at the low range for my anti coagulation. Maybe only another day or two of lovenox shots.

Had a visitor today from the church. Tom and I had a very nice visit and he went out and got me a Big Mac meal. Tomorrow my parents will be coming down.

With trying to move houses Amanda couldn't come down this weekend. I miss her so much. I may not see her until I am transported home, but she has so much going on I will survive.

That's about it for today. Again thank you for your prayers and support.

Steve

July 31, 2016 ·

For some reason again today during OT my heart rate dropped from 120's to 70's. All I did was six minutes on a hand bike. This really needs to stop as I don't want this to delay me going home.

My parents visited today and brought me a bean burrito and Mountain Dew from Taco Bell.

The weekends here are pretty mellow and for some reason I got another headache. Not as bad as last week but still a drag.

Scheduled to come home in four days. Pray that I will be ready and that it's not premature.

Have a great night and if you have time this week and want to help prepare our new house you can check out one of yesterday's posts that gives that info
Steve

August 1, 2016 ·
Please pray. Not feeling well. Very fatigued. Steve.

August 2, 2016 ·
Yesterday I couldn't really do PT or OT. My body felt really miserable. I napped in morning and the afternoon and slept fairly descent last night.

Today I am back to normal. Had good therapy sessions but no so good food. That's one of the biggest trials is I am not enjoying the food. Same stuff.

Anyhow, since I am feeling better and if tomorrow is the same I get to go home Thursday. I cry every time I think about it. It's been 67 days since my aortic dissection and home sounds sooooo good.

Please continue to pray for strength and no complications. It's going to stretch me to come home but I believe I will get stronger quicker.
Steve

August 3, 2016 ·
As of right now I had my last PT & OT sessions down here at Lifecare today. The rehab sessions will shift to home care and then I'll probably go to our local rehab center.

It will be unreal to go home tomorrow after nearly 10 weeks. I still have a long way to go but getting home will definitely be a nice transition.

Thank you for your prayers and the scores who have helped with our new house. Looking to move on Saturday.

Next post from me will hopefully come from Seneca, PA!
Steve

August 4, 2016 ·
Home

Here's a handful of other significant Facebook posts from this point forward

August 5, 2016 ·
Well, I've been home for almost 24 hours. I've eaten more these last hours then I had the previous 2-3 days. (Sausage gravy and biscuits, corn on the cob, Stromboli, and a can of spaghetti O's.)

Getting stronger and VNA came in today. I also tested my INR (how thin my blood is) and its 2.6 which is in range which means no more Lovenox shots! PTL

Looking forward to a visit tomorrow by a friend from out of town.

Please continue to pray and remember for those local we are NOT moving tomorrow. It's another work day at our new house. Feel free to come out to the new house if you have a couple hours. Love you - Steve

August 6, 2016 ·
Left lung a little gunky today. I'll be using my breathing apparatus a lot today and trying to cough up as much as I can. Feel free to pray for my lung to clear. I truly believe that I am only alive because of your prayers so a gunky lung is nothing. -Steve

August 6, 2016 · Post from Todd – UB Bishop
I had a great visit with Steve and Amanda Henry today at their home. Steve is healing more each and every day. Thankful that the Lord has generously provided for the Henry family. Grateful for a praying UB family of churches that intercedes beyond their local church interests and issues. #UBlessed#UBenefits

August 8, 2016 ·
Had a good day yesterday. I was able to go to our church's Car Cruise. I don't think I've ever been hugged so much, but it was great. So nice to see people who have been praying for me.

We had 175 vehicles, a new record, and fed 325 people.

Sadly I didn't sleep well last. My mind just kept very active. That's my biggest concern is that I'm not sleeping we'll.

Pain wise things aren't too bad I just want to sleep through the night.

Getting stronger everyday which is nice. Able to stand up easier and walking isn't taking as much out of me as last week.

VNA will be in today and maybe PT and OT. Just chomping to get back to strength.

A house update should be coming later today so stay tuned.
Steve

August 9, 2016 ·
Super excited because Amanda is going to call to make sure we own my walker and that it's not just rented.

If it's mine I'm going to name it. Wanna guess my walkers name? I'm going to name it "Texas Ranger".

If you don't get it I don't know what to say.

August 13, 2016 ·

Today's the day! I can't believe it. We are moving to our new house this morning. We have been so blessed by all those who have prepped our new house and helped us pack. Thanks! ~Amanda

August 14, 2016 ·

Went to church today. A time of tears and cheers. Great to be there. Slight mistake by going out to eat for lunch. . . Had to be taken home before we finished.

Felt pretty lousy after that. (Happy I was able to eat some tasty frog legs though)

90 minute nap which helped but my left side still hurts pretty bad. Had X-rays on Friday to check for rib injury or scaring of my lung.

We moved into our new house yesterday. It's so much bigger! Nearly 100 people over the last three weeks made it possible. It's overwhelming the love we have been freely given.

I wish I could roam our 28 acres and such, but that work will have to wait until 2017.

Thank you to all who have prayed, volunteered your time, and those who blessed us with financial gifts.

God is good
Steve.

August 25, 2016 ·

CT done and I saw Dr Chess my endograph surgeon. The CT looked good. No fluid anywhere and the piece they put in looked good. All clear from surgeon perspective.

Now it's just getting my strength back and trying to be more active.

August 27, 2016 ·

It was 3 months ago today that our lives were flipped upside down. I knew immediately on May 27 that my aorta had dissected. The pain was intense and I assumed that I was going to meet Jesus face to face soon.

Apparently that wasn't in His plans. I can't believe it's been three months. So many prayers. So much pain for so many people. Numerous times I wanted to die. I pleaded with God to stop my heart so the pain would be gone. He said "No."

It's been a hard journey that still has weeks/months for a full recovery. Ups and downs. The limitations still are difficult to come to grips with. The pain and fatigue do get tiresome but that will pass.

My outlook on life is definitely a little different now.

So thankful for Amanda for being my rock when I was completely empty.

Also thankful for the prayers and help of hundreds of people.

Still learning,
Steve

137

September 1, 2016 ·
I feel like so many of you are journeying with me over these months. Had two good appointments today. I started with a counselor/psychologist and I really like her. I will go weekly and hopefully I'll be able to process through the trauma of the last three months.

Then I was able to get to the doctors and they are starting me on two meds that will hopefully help with the anxiety/panic attacks.

I guess I needed to come to the point where I need professional guidance and help. I look forward to continued healing and your continued prayers and love mean so much.

Steve

September 4, 2016 ·
Steve has been home 4 weeks and had a great report from his surgeon and his cardiologist the end of August. Unfortunately, somewhere along the way he picked up pneumonia again.

I took him to his Dr's office Saturday evening and they wanted him to go to the ER because some things medically weren't looking good. They did an X-ray and he has a moderate case of pneumonia. They wanted to send him to Pittsburgh but he asked to stay here locally. He is being admitted tonight and will start IV meds.

Thank you for your prayers and support along this journey. ~Amanda

September 5, 2016 ·
I'm currently having my sixth or seventh infusion of antibiotics for pneumonia. I was moved to the ICU yesterday morning at UPMC Northwest as we are hoping this can be treated close to home and me not having to go to Pittsburgh.

Honestly I am feeling better. Breathing especially. Please pray for my mind to be clear and that my lungs will clear up quickly. Trying not to be discouraged, Steve.

September 6, 2016 ·
Well a lot seems to be going on. I am being moved back to a regular room but my shortness of breath continues. An echocardiogram was done this morning and it was found that my actual heart isn't functioning how it should. This was probably caused by all the trauma over the last three months.

Your heart is supposed to pump out roughly 50% of the blood that goes is in. Mine is currently at 27%. They believe it can be treated but pray please.

Pneumonia is clearing but heart is concern as well as intense panic and anxiety.

Steve.

138

September 10, 2016 ·
It's been a few days since an update. I traveled via ambulance to Allegheny General Hospital last night. The pneumonia is getting better but I wanted to get to my docs when it comes to my heart function.

Don't know a whole lot other then I'd rather be at home. Trusting my heart will get stronger.

Steve

September 14, 2016 ·
The docs couldn't pinpoint why my heart function decreased causing the fluid buildup so they let me come home. I have to wear a LifeVest which will shock me back if I go into A-Fib. It's quite uncomfortable to wear across my back and chest but with a heart that's functioning in the mid 20% range if I need a jump start I'm ok with that.

On a few new meds to really keep heart rate low. Of course a low salt diet (I was never a big salt fan anyway) and it's back trying to get into productive shape again. 80 days in the hospital this year I'd sure like to not add anymore to that number.

Good to be home
Steve

September 20, 2016 ·
Well we made a trip to Pittsburgh today to see my cardiologist. He's very concerned that my ejection fraction (percentage of blood being pumped out of heart) dropped to the mid 20% range.

He clearly stated that three weeks ago that I didn't have pneumonia but it was all congestive heart failure. Marfan Syndrome does not cause this and its origin as to why my heart muscle is weak is unknown.

I'm on another medication to help strengthen my heart and I will be starting cardiac rehab soon. If my ejection fraction doesn't improve in three months or so we will be looking at some potential surgical procedures to implant some things on my heart.

If things continue to decrease with the ejection fraction then we may have to cross the road of heart transplant, but that's worst case scenario. I would prefer keeping my heart!

Gonna trust that my ejection fraction will improve and nothing needs to be "installed" inside of me. Lol

Steve

September 21, 2016 ·
Blood pressure meds a little too much. BP 65/36
We're adjusting. I'm sleepy. Nurse amazed I'm still awake. Lol

October 8, 2016 ·

Tomorrow is a big day for me. It will be 140 days since I last preached at Victory Heights. Of those 140 days, 80 of them were in the hospital or rehab. I still honestly haven't grasped all that has happened over these days. (You are all welcome to come out at 10:30AM)

Now in congestive heart failure it's one day at a time. We just scheduled another heart cath, cardiac MRI, and stress test for November 10th and we should know definitively if I am getting better, staying the same, or getting worse.

It will be nice to do what God has called me to do again starting tomorrow. Hopefully for those local you can join us tomorrow to celebrate the grace, faithfulness, and healing that only God can give.

Our sermon title is "Endurance + Encouragement = Unity"
Love you,
Steve

November 9, 2016 ·

Having Steve with me still is truly a miracle. We head to Pittsburgh today for early testing tomorrow trying to place the cause and extent of his heart failure.

We would appreciate your prayers. Not just for the Dr's to not see anything wrong but that if there is a problem for the Dr's to see it. I want nothing hidden that is present but instead I pray for healing or wisdom in diagnosis and treatment. Thank you and may we all remember how big God is. ~Amanda

November 11, 2016 ·

Well, today was my all day testing at Allegheny General Hospital. Amanda and I spent the night last night at the hotel that she spent many nights alone while I was in the hospital this summer.

I had a stress test at 8am and then got a hospital room to await my other two tests. After waiting till nearly 1pm they finally took me for a heart cath through my neck. That was not very enjoyable and I have to keep the bandage on till tomorrow.

I was then taken for a cardiac MRI, but after the first preliminary scan it was determined that I couldn't have it done. The endograph (the piece put in this summer to fix my dissection) has a spring type makeup and that metal prevented the MRI to be clear. So sadly I can never have that test done and that MRI was going to give us a good heart function measurement.

The doctor came in and informed us that my stress test results were poor and that my heart cath findings weren't too encouraging either. Not really what we were hoping for but we've come this far and I know that God is still good.

I have to continue to wear my LifeVest till January when I will have an echocardiogram done to check my heart function. If my heart function isn't 35% or greater in January then a permanent defibrillator/pacemaker will be surgically implanted shortly thereafter. The docs sounded as if I will need to ready for that due to today's test results.

140

I will be starting cardio rehab soon though since I have today's test results. Hopefully that will help me regain some stamina regardless of the poor heart function.

That's my update. No worries, just one day at a time. God's got it under control and I'll just continue to learn lessons through it all.

In Him,

Steve

December 1, 2016 ·

I start cardiac rehab at 8am today. Will go 3x/week for the next three months. Not particularly looking forward to it, but hopefully it will help me regain some more strength and stamina. -Steve

January 27, 2017 ·

Heading to Pittsburgh for an echocardiogram and to see the heart failure doctors. Our prayer is that my heart function is at 35% or greater. Your prayers for today would be greatly appreciated. - Steve

January 28, 2017 ·

An hour ago we received an email with "Test Results". After any test or procedure an email comes through with the medical terminology results.

It was the results of Friday's echocardiogram. It's a mixed bag that isn't as good as we were hoping. My heart function (ejection fraction) is only at 30%. It was between 20-24% five months ago so there has been an improvement which is encouraging.

I'm sure the doctor will call us on Monday to make sure that I keep my LifeVest on for some more time. I'll probably have another echocardiogram in 3 or so months to see where my EF is, but for now it appears that my LifeVest will be a part of my life for a little while longer.

Just as I told the kids the other day we have to have the faith and belief in God like Shadrach, Meshach, & Abednego. He can chose to save (heal) us from the fire but if we have to go in it He will be right there with us. I wanted to hit 35% heart function yesterday but it didn't happen. That doesn't change my trust and hope in the Lord. PERIOD

To all my FB friends use each day to the fullest. Life changes but God never does. Live each day with a heart (regardless of its function) sold out for Christ. - Steve

February 7, 2017 ·

Tonight was a milestone night and an oops night. First the milestone. Tonight I grilled hamburgers and hot dogs for the first time in 9 months. Our grill needed a new flame guard that I purchased two months ago but it hadn't been put in the grill.

When I opened the trunk of the car the new guard was laying on top with the walker I had to use for a few months underneath.

After getting the grill fixed and getting meat on I walked back into the house and asked Amanda to come over. I hugged her and started to cry because it had been so long since I could do this. I don't care about who won the Super Bowl or who our President is, I'm happy to be able do more of life again. (All enjoyed supper too)

On the oops side, I took my evening pills this morning and just took my morning pills 10 minutes ago. The oops part is that I take a pill in the morning called Bumex. It's a water pill. Now I get to use the toilet for the next 3-4 hours while my fluid is coming off. I wanted to go to bed by 10:30 too. Yikes! - Steve

That evening of grilling was one of the many milestones that have been accomplished since that mild February evening. Since then I have been able to build a raised garden box, mow the yard, cut a little bit of wood, and even break out a slab of cement with a sledgehammer! There are many accomplishments and milestones yet to come, but glory must be given to God for His care and love for me and my family.

Unfortunately, my heart function didn't increase much more in 2017 and I did end up having a pacemaker/defibrillator implanted in May of 2017. Sadly, it misfired three times in July (which was not enjoyable at all feeling like one is hit with a baseball bat square in the back), and I had another one implanted differently two days after the misfires.

I know that this chapter was odd, but so many families journey through difficult times that I felt that Amanda's viewpoints and reactions would be very insightful. This was the most difficult time in our lives, and these updates only scratched the surface of the hardship of those days. The most important element within these updates is the fact that it was God's strength and the prayers of thousands that gave us strength. This story very well could have had a different ending if it wasn't for those prayers.

Cherish every day that you are blessed to live. Never waste the valuable time that you have with your loved ones. Life can change at a moments notice without any preparations.

eleven

ACCEPTING YOUR SCARS

Emotional and physical scars often shape a variety of aspects in our lives. Recalling and remembering those pivotal scar-producing moments isn't easy either. Those scars are part of our essence, part of who we are at the core, but we all have to decide how those *Custom Scars* will be used. Are you willing to use them for the positive, which can leave you vulnerable, or do you close yourself off and try to bear the scars alone? That choice is in front of us daily.

For example, two years after my heart valve tore (remember December 2010) I was visiting a parishioner in our local hospital. (This is the same hospital where I was taken initially after my aortic valve tear and dissection.) While I was in the room visiting the parishioner, one of the nurses who had seen me in the hall thought she remembered me. She walked into the room and asked me if I was the patient with the major heart issue a couple of years prior. I described the day and the situation and then she looked straight into my eyes and soberly said that she and the other emergency room staff didn't believe that I would survive because of my rapid deterioration. Just my being there and alive was not only proof to her of my survival but it gave me an opportunity to thank her for her part and to also give God the glory for His strength and mercy during that difficult trial.

Regardless of your age or social demographics, it's guaranteed that you have scars. Whether it's from your childhood, teenage years, young adult life, and even older and hopefully wiser years, it is a fact of life that scars will always continue to accumulate. This world is full of evil and sin. Scars happen because we live in a fallen world and that's why hope is needed.

The questions each of us must personally answer are these: When *Custom Scars* present themselves, what do I do about them? How do I react to them? Do I let them take control?

Maybe the real question is the one I have alluded to throughout this book: Am I going to allow my scars to define who I am? Are the scars going to control me, or am I going to use them to move forward and even help others find hope?

When I am at the store or at the mall, people typically look twice at me and often whisper to each other loud enough for me to hear them say, "Man, he's tall!" Sometimes the whisperings are subtle, while other times they can be quite annoying. I'm always dumbfounded when people come right up to me and say, "Boy, you're tall." Do they believe I don't know this each day when I wake up and look at myself in the mirror? Trust me, I know I'm tall.

Being as tall as I am is a symptom of Marfan syndrome. It can have its negative moments, but I truly do enjoy being tall. I often take advantage of my height when people ask questions about my basketball career. That career never occurred, but it gives me a great opportunity to share the things I can do and the miracles that have occurred in my life. Pointing them toward God and the hope that He has given to me despite my scars probably wasn't the direction they intended the conversation to go when asking about basketball!

My physical scars can be hidden fairly easily. People can't see the six-plus feet of scars that my clothes conceal. They will probably never experience the feeling of having even one chest tube pulled, let alone a dozen. While my *Custom Scars* aren't evident to people I meet each day, I not only see each one of them every morning, but I also hear them.

The new heart valve that was grafted in 2010 ticks and it ticks loudly. Due to the thinness of my chest, I literally hear my valve working with each and every heartbeat. My heart beats about eighty-five beats per minute, or 44.6 million beats per year, so I hear a lot of ticking. It's a continual reminder of the gratefulness for the life that God has given me. You can't get away from the beating of your heart!

For years Amanda has depended on my *Custom Scars* to help her sleep at night. That ticking helps her sleep now. If I'm out of town for the night, she puts a ticking clock on my pillow so she can sleep, and she takes one with her if she happens to be out without me.

A pastor friend, Bill Hastings, sat beside me at a prayer meeting a while back where people could lead out in prayer if they felt led. When a prayer service flows like that, often times there are periods of silence when no one is praying. When it's quiet, the ticking of my valve seems to be the loudest sound in the room! A few days after the prayer meeting, I saw Bill again. He asked, "Was that your heart ticking that I heard during our prayer meeting a few days ago?" I chuckled and told him it was indeed my valve hard at work.

It can be a little bothersome hearing the ticking all the time. Playing hide-and-seek with the kids can be hard because if it is too quiet, the kids just listen and dad's ticker will give away his hiding place!

The only scar not typically covered by clothes is on the back of my head and neck where I had brain surgery. Since I am so tall, not many people ever see it either. My cut-off finger isn't really evident to people because it's still longer than most people's full-length index finger.

Maybe you want to hide your scars. Some of us can hide them easily, while others can't. Everyone is scarred but just in different places! Too often we spend our lives hiding both our physical and

Everyone is scarred but just in different places!

emotional scars because they remind us of some hurt or pain. I know I've tried to hide my hurt. When I was younger, I tried to hide my emotional scars behind humor. My mom encouraged me to just laugh with the kids when they teased me, saying they would stop because it wasn't getting them anywhere. While laughing sometimes made the teasing stop, it never took away the pain. You have probably laughed on the outside while you were crying out for help, love, and acceptance on the inside. I can completely understand the desire to keep one's scars hidden.

Amanda and I are doing our best to teach all our children to accept their own scars and the scars of others. I will never be able to remove my scars or wash them off. Honestly, they are a reminder to me each day of the privilege I have to even be alive. The scars I wake up to each day and the ticking that never stops enable me to survive. The scars motivate me to be the husband, father, and pastor God has called me to be. They help me realize that life is short. In a scoop of snow on a December morning or the rinsing of soap, life could be gone.

147

I make it a point to walk around the house in warm weather with my shirt off for two reasons. The first one is obvious: it's hot. The other is to try to help teach my children that people who seem to be "different" are really the same! My children see my scars and see that I have accepted them, and I live each day to the fullest regardless. I let them touch my scars to know that, although things might look different or feel different, I am still their dad.

As I have mentioned, two of our three boys have Marfan syndrome. I want to teach and lead them to know that God made them exactly the way He wants them to be. I encourage them continually that they are like their dad and it's my responsibility to provide them with a role model that exemplifies strength, acceptance, perseverance, character, and hope.

One of my sons, Dylan, has a very concave chest. The kids at school have asked him about it. I told him that he was created this way and that God doesn't make mistakes. He accepts that answer without question, and accepts his uniqueness because he sees and knows that I believe it and live it. He trusts his father. I will always speak the truth to him about his uniqueness regardless of the scars that come his way. As he's getting older, this is becoming more challenging, but I have to be consistent and help guide him in all seasons of life.

I love it when we go to the beach or pool with the kids because the boys take their shirts off and don't care that they may look different than the other boys around. When I was young, my mother discouraged me from taking my shirt off because my chest was also very concave and she wanted to protect me from being teased. Instead, I needed my parents to tell me and encourage me that God

148

created me exactly how I was supposed to be according to His plan for my life. That is what Amanda and I need to pass down to all our children regardless of their physical conditions. Our children are exactly how God wants them to be. As parents we must love and do all we can for our children so they know beyond a shadow of a doubt that they are loved regardless of their *Custom Scars*.

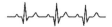

How do the scars that are part of your life affect you? Do they control you, or have you been able to use them to help others? When I see someone who is bound to a wheelchair, I think about the stares that person receives because his or her scars are evident. I also see so many loving parents whose children are bound to wheelchairs who love them with a passionate, self-sacrificing love. My heart breaks when I see or hear people treat those who have severe physical limitations without respect. I imagine that some days they wish they could hide their scars, but that has never been possible for them. I can easily hide my scars, and you would probably treat me like any other person. But how do you treat those who cannot hide their scars?

Maybe you were born with a genetic condition, perhaps some type of speech or stamina trouble. Maybe you were in an accident and have lost a limb or become disfigured. Maybe you have emotional scars that carry the same weight as a physical scar. No matter which scars you have, you have been given a choice. You can let those scars control you or you can have hope that you can use those scars for the betterment of yourself and those with whom you come in contact.

How can people not be controlled by their *Custom Scars*? I've not been able to make it in my own strength, but have fully relied on the strength from God. When I speak to groups about my genetic condition, my faith always comes up. I don't compartmentalize it into one section of my life and my genetic condition into another because they cannot be separated. Rather, my faith enables me to be hopeful and to accept my scars. I know God doesn't make mistakes. I AM NOT A MISTAKE! YOU ARE NOT A MISTAKE!

I know the media, magazines, movies, and television seem to tell us that we have to look or act a certain way to be acceptable. All that rubbish being fed to us needs to be thrown back into the trash from whence it came. God made you special. He accepts you and your scars.

God made you special. He accepts you and your scars.

Remember that doctor who told me, when I was twelve years old, that I was a freak mutation? To God, I was never a freak or a mutation. I was exactly the way He wanted me to be. That is where I ultimately receive the vision and passion to accept my *Custom Scars*. Romans 8:37 says, "In all these things we are more than conquerors through Him [Jesus] who loved us." This acceptance comes from knowing that the God who created the universe made me exactly how He wants me to be. Through Jesus I can handle life's battles with hope.

As a pastor, I visit many people who are sick and dying. Often, they ask me why they are still alive. "What can I do in this state?" they ask. They know they are dying, so why not just speed things up? I listen to them, sometimes cry with them, then reassure them that God is in control and in His time our present suffering will be over. I let them know that if their continuance in life is only for me to be able to visit with them, I would hope it would be worth it. No matter what your scars are, God loves you.

My faith, being a Christian, gives me immeasurable hope that God has a plan for me that is greater than I can imagine. I have drawn hope from the Bible and the many promises God has given me about how He cares for everyone. King David even wrote in Psalm 139 that God was concerned for us before we were born! If He cared about us

> **The scars in our lives have never surprised God. He is right there waiting for you to rely on Him to carry you.**

before we were born, don't you think He cares just as much for us after we are born? When God was knitting me together in my mother's womb, He knew I would have Marfan syndrome, yet this psalm still applies to me. When God was knitting Dylan and Andrew together inside Amanda's womb, this psalm applied to them, too! No matter what your *Custom Scars* may be, this psalm is all about you. God made me and you exactly the way He intended us to be. The scars in our lives have never surprised God. He is right there waiting for you to rely on Him to carry you.

He desires to use the scars in your life to help others. The scars we were born with, the scars we endure throughout life, and the scars we die with never catch God off guard. He never stops loving us!

We often suppress painful memories. Hopefully reading *Custom Scars* was a reminder that our scars aren't to control us. Life can be tough and you may want to give up, but I want to encourage you to stay strong, seek out a supportive friend, and talk to God about it.

twelve

THE SCARS THAT SAVE

Custom Scars began with a passage from the Bible written by the Apostle Paul to the church in the city of Corinth. He was talking about the many memorable trials and scars he had endured. These weren't scars he was born with, but scars that occurred because he was sharing the love of Jesus in towns, cities, and the world. Paul wanted the Christians in Corinth to understand he freely accepted his scars in order for people to learn more and have the opportunity to accept the love and forgiveness of Jesus.

I think about all the experiences that have produced my *Custom Scars*, particularly the times when I felt life wasn't worth living and I just wanted to give up. I would then read passages of Scripture, words of history, and I felt humbled at how minimal my scars actually are. I read of Paul's *Custom Scars* and his perseverance for the cause of Christ and then ask myself, *What am I doing with my Custom Scars for Jesus? How do my sufferings compare to Paul's?* Paul says in 2 Corinthians 11:23b-28,

> "I have worked much harder, been in prison more frequently, been flogged more severely, and been exposed to death again and again. Five times I received from the Jews the forty lashes minus one. Three times I was beaten with rods, once I was stoned, three times I was shipwrecked, I spent a night and a day in the open sea, I have been constantly on the move. I have been in danger from rivers, in danger from bandits, in danger from my own countrymen, in danger from Gentiles; in danger in the city, in danger in the country, in danger at sea; and in danger from false brothers. I have labored and toiled and have often

152

gone without sleep; I have known hunger and thirst and have often gone without food; I have been cold and naked. Besides everything else, I face daily the pressure of my concern for all the churches. Who is weak, and I do not feel weak? Who is led into sin, and I do not inwardly burn?"

A few verses later, in 2 Corinthians 12:9, Paul hears Jesus saying to him, "My grace is sufficient for you, for my power is made perfect in weakness." That, my friend, is a promise from God that even though my *Custom Scars* affect my life, God's power is perfect and greater than any scar. His power for your life is greater than any scar you may deal with too.

I have not been subjected to even one iota of the scars inflicted upon Paul. He was jailed, whipped, beaten with rods, stoned, shipwrecked, and more. The one section in this passage that has affected me the most is verse 24, "Five times I received from the Jews the forty lashes minus one." They were not allowed to inflict forty lashes, because they believed forty lashes were more than a human body could withstand. This probably refers to using what was called a cat-o'-nine-tails, where nine separate pieces of leather were connected to the end of a whip. Pieces of bone or metal on those strips would rip the flesh from the person being lashed.

Five different times, Paul received this punishment for telling others about Jesus. I don't believe you or I can even fathom what his back, chest, legs, or arms looked like after he was given 195 lashes. If the instrument of his lashings was indeed the dreaded cat-o'-nine-tails, then his body would have been ravaged by 1,755 separate tears and perforations. Jesus had this done to Him once, and it is written in Scripture that He was unrecognizable.

153

Paul withstood his *Custom Scars* the same way that you and I can withstand ours. The grace of God is sufficient for us, and God makes us perfect in our weaknesses. Our hope comes from the Lord. He will provide the strength for us to deal with our *Custom Scars* because He did not make any mistakes in creating us.

Paul sustained those types of scars solely for his belief and love for Jesus. What could be so powerful in a person's life that he or she would be willing to suffer so much? Why would someone keep heaping scars upon themselves for what they believe? Shouldn't Paul have just given up? Was it really worth it?

I have asked those same questions about myself while I was enduring my various procedures and hospitalizations. But then I look at this one man, Paul, and see that his scars surpass mine and probably those of every person reading this book. He never stopped sharing with people what he believed about the hope and love that can only come through accepting Jesus.

Paul kept teaching and preaching what he believed, even though his scars were too numerous to count. Again, I ask myself, *What am I willing to do with the scars in my life?* If I am wonderfully made by God, then these scars have been given to me for a reason, just as Paul's scars were given to him for a reason. Your scars are a part of your life for a reason. Even when scars are intended for evil, God can heal them and use them to help others.

I want to be straightforward that the title of this chapter, "The Scars That Save," doesn't refer to the scars on my body or on your body. Although the scars on the Apostle Paul were many, his scars are not the ones that can save. The only scars that save are the ones that came from Jesus Christ, God's Son.

154

Not only does God love me, but He gave His Son, Jesus, to offer me forgiveness, hope, and eternal life in Heaven. Jesus had many scars inflicted on His body, even though He did not deserve a single one of them. He was simply willing to be scarred for us. The scars Jesus took for us are the only ones that can truly give us life.

Jesus was raised in a simple community called Nazareth where He grew up like all the other kids around Him. I imagine His mom and dad did the typical things that parents did during this time period. So Jesus grew up knowing how to work hard and lived a typical Jewish life near family and friends. He would have attended the local synagogue each Sabbath throughout His childhood. Jesus would have suffered scars from His early life just as we do. It is traditionally believed that His earthly father, Joseph, died while Jesus was still young. He knew what it was like to hurt and be hurt. He cried when He hurt, just like we do. He had similar scars.

It wasn't until Jesus was thirty years old that He began to teach and preach a message of hope for the hurting. He went throughout the region, with twelve men He chose as His close companions, preaching and teaching that He was the Messiah who had been prophesied. Throughout His three years of earthly ministry, Jesus healed many people's scars. He made the blind to see, the lame to walk, the deaf to hear and the lepers to be clean. He even raised people from the dead. Jesus knew people had physical, emotional, and spiritual scars and He is the only One who can completely heal any scar in your life.

Since Jesus came from heaven to earth and was born to the virgin Mary, He is the only One who has ever walked this planet and never done anything wrong. We have a perfect man, Jesus, who was falsely accused, beaten, and hung to die on a cross after just three years of ministry. Jesus, the only perfect man who ever lived, didn't die for Himself, however; He died for you and me. He took my sins and my scars and died for them.

Not only did the death of Jesus on that Roman cross give everyone in the entire world the opportunity to be forgiven of his or her sins, it also gave us the opportunity to trust in the One who loves us just as we are. Jesus died for me . . . this scarred person. He not only loves me unconditionally, He accepts my scars unconditionally. I have willfully laid my life at the feet of the One who took the scars of my sin on His shoulders. John 3:16 says, "For God so loved the world that he gave his one and only son, that whoever believes in him shall not perish but have eternal life." The "whoever" is you and me, regardless of the scars in our lives. Hope, healing, and salvation are available through Jesus alone.

My faith as a Christian is not about religion. It is about a relationship with the One who suffered and died to take and forgive my sins. I have the freedom to share, love, and encourage people regarding their *Custom Scars*. Despite my scars, I am wonderfully made just how God wants me to be.

The things I just spoke of about Jesus might be totally foreign to you. You may have never heard anything about Jesus, but He is the One upon whom history is based. Jesus was born into this world to give all of us scarred people eternal life in Heaven.

He allowed Himself to carry my scars on the cross with Him. If the story ended there, we wouldn't have any hope, but the story continues as Jesus did not stay dead. He came back to life. Because He came back to life, He conquered sin and death for us. All we have to do is believe in Him for the forgiveness that is free. Do you want the hope that comes through Jesus? That choice is yours alone.

Jesus has the scars of the nail marks on His hands and feet where He was nailed to a cross. He also has the scars of where He was pierced by a spear on His side. Jesus endured those scars for you and for me. I would not be able to look toward the future with confidence and hope if it wasn't for the fact that I have allowed God to be in control of my life.

I want to share one last story with you before you get to "The End" of *Custom Scars*. During my days in the hospital while I was battling my aortic dissection, bleeding ulcers, and lung distress I truly believe that I got a taste of Heaven. I don't know how or why, but I remember being somewhere (no bright lights or Saint Peter jingling the keys of Heaven in front of me) and having a sense of peace, love, and contentment that is indescribable.

Never, as far as anyone knows, did I actually flatline, but when I was able to speak to Amanda that next time, I told her that if I got really bad to just let me go because I got a taste of Heaven. My heart longed to go back there. Philippians 4:7 says, "And the peace of God, which transcends all understanding, will guard your hearts and your minds in Christ Jesus." Although we look at this verse as dealing with the here and now, I was able to experience that peace that no words can describe. No words can convey that peace, but when it's my time to reach eternity, I know that there is no other place that I would rather be.

No matter what scars come my way, Jesus will see me safely through and it's with that hope that I am grateful for my *Custom Scars*.

AFTERWORD

Steve Henry opens the door to a sacred entrance into his life and invites the reader into a journey of roller coaster emotions, and a victorious adventure on the steady road of perseverance. Steve candidly and vividly shares his struggles and reveals his seeming defeats, all leading to a powerfully victorious conclusion; God ordains and customizes the scars in our lives, large and small, deep and shallow, for His righteous and loving purposes.

Custom Scars powerfully brings love of God and love of family to light. It speaks of one man's determination to succeed and overcome physical and emotional tribulation. Its words vividly remind us of hope and purpose as precious individuals in God's treasured creation. It reminds us to count each moment we live as a gift to be cherished and used wisely.

Reading *Custom Scars* brought me to those places in my personal life that are simply uncomfortable. Though my hurts and struggles pale in comparison to Steve's, the effects and challenges of my custom scars are real, and Steve's story has caused me to rethink my own life's wounds and look at them afresh in light of God's love and purpose for my journey through life.

I recommend *Custom Scars* to those who wrestle with their physical, emotional, and spiritual challenges. I also recommend this book to pastors who deal with congregations full of "custom scars".

I endorse this book to be read by families who are suffering over their children's physical limitations brought about by the heartache of health problems.

But beyond these recommendations, and perhaps even more vital in this generation, I recommend Steve Henry's *Custom Scars* to young people who suffer the consequences of harboring a "hard heart" toward others in an increasing callous world, with hopes that Steve's story will soften them and produce in them a good measure of compassion and mercy.

-Wayne Taylor
General Manager - Mars Hill Network - Syracuse, NY

Romans 5:3-5

"Not only so, but we also rejoice in our sufferings, because we know that suffering produces perseverance; perseverance, character; and character, hope. And <u>hope</u> does not disappoint us, because God has poured out his love into our hearts by the Holy Spirit, whom he has given us."

To schedule a speaking engagement for your church, medical school/facility, pregnancy center, or conference please send all correspondence to customscars@yahoo.com or fill in the form on www.customscars.org.

If you have more questions about Marfan syndrome or faith in Jesus, please visit www.customscars.org.

Email: customscars@yahoo.com
Facebook: www.facebook.com/MarfanScars/

Made in the USA
Middletown, DE
20 November 2018